Wrestling

WITH THE

Restoration

Wrestling

WITH THE

Restoration

WHY THIS
CHURCH MATTERS

STEVEN C. HARPER

DESERET
BOOK

Salt Lake City, Utah

Library of Congress Cataloging-in-Publication Data
(CIP data on file)

ISBN 978-1-63993-362-4

Printed in the United States of America
Publishers Printing

10   9   8   7   6   5   4   3   2   1

Lovingly dedicated to Scott,
who ably took the helm
when the captain abandoned the ship.

And to Hannah Marie,
who saw the ship and its precious passengers
safely to the promised land.

And to all aboard,
who could have mutinied
but chose to minister instead.
This is lovingly dedicated to you
for cheerfully making the stormy maiden voyage.

Also to Martha, who visited twice.

And to The Queen, who never left.

And to Ruth and Andrew,
who both love Andrew's favorite hymn
because the King is the same as the answer.
And the answer is always . . .

Contents

CONTENTS

STARTING RIGHT

1.

Think Slow

This book is supposed to do two kinds of work. One is to inform readers what the Restoration is and does and why it matters. The other is to encourage readers to become better at knowing what they know about the Restoration and how they know it. This is why:

The psychologist Daniel Kahneman wrote the book *Thinking Fast and Slow*.[1] It's the result of a massive amount of research he and others did, showing how humans use mental shortcuts called heuristics to make decisions. That is thinking fast. It is biased. For example, when a hundred people are asked if they are an above average driver, almost all of them answer *yes*. Sports analysts get paid to think fast—to offer on-the-spot explanations for why a team or a player performed the way they did: too much time off, too little time off, home court advantage, being unified against a hostile crowd. Thinking fast creates the sense that we know things that we really do not know. We often think we are reaching rational conclusions when we are actually relying on heuristics for explanations that satisfy us.

But these stories we tell ourselves would not survive scrutiny because they are not knowledge. They are illusions of knowledge.

Thinking fast is effortless. It is easier on our brains than thinking slowly. Experts think too fast sometimes. People who are not experts think too fast when they assume that whatever an expert or Internet source says is true. Thinking fast may be benign for sports fans. But it is unwise and potentially devastating to think fast about ultimate things, about truth—about God, Christ, the restored gospel, Church history, prophets. So if, like Joseph Smith, you are a person who considers it vital to be right "in matters that involve eternal consequences," then thinking slowly is for you.[2]

Thinking slowly requires effort. It demands sustained attention and concentration. But it is deeply rewarding and—with enough practice—it can become habitual. My students and I practice the hard work of slowing down when we think about ultimate things. When combined with faith in Jesus Christ, a sincere heart, and real intent, thinking slowly contributes to resilient, mature faith, hope, and charity that resist and repel assaults and attacks.

Thinking slowly begins by thinking about what and how we think, or metacognition. When we analyze our thoughts, we are metacognitive. I ask my students what they know and how they know it, and we read together from the earliest source documents of the Restoration because source awareness is part of thinking slowly—or metacognitively—about what we know and how we know it. What are the sources of our knowledge? How do they know what they say they know? Seeking answers to source-related questions is called source criticism.

We start off each semester practicing source criticism with Joseph Smith's 1832 history. It is six pages, mostly in his handwriting. What we know about the Restoration and how we know it is bound up in this document and others like it. We think about them slowly while seeking to know in what ways they are reliable sources of knowledge and in what ways they are not. That requires knowing all that can be known about who created them and when and why and how.

Moroni's well-known method for knowing ultimate things teaches us to combine slow thinking source criticism with faithful yearning. There are six ingredients in Moroni's recipe for knowing. Notice how the first three teach us to think slowly:

> Behold, I would exhort you that when ye shall *read these things*, if it be wisdom in God that ye should read them, that ye would *remember how merciful the Lord hath been* unto the children of men, from the creation of Adam even down until the time that ye shall receive these things, and *ponder it in your hearts.* (Moroni 10:3; emphasis added)

Then notice what happens when we add three ingredients of spiritual work to the brain work:

> And when ye shall receive these things, I would exhort you that ye would ask God, the Eternal Father, in the name of Christ, if these things are not true; and if ye shall ask with a *sincere heart,* with *real intent,* having *faith in Christ,* he will manifest the truth of it unto you, by the power of the Holy Ghost. And by the power of the Holy Ghost ye may know the truth of all things. (Moroni 10:4–5; emphasis added)

This is a highly contingent promise, especially the if/then clause preceding the spiritual work: *if* we ask with a sincere heart, real intent, and faith in Christ, *then* He will reveal the truth to us by the Holy Ghost. It all hangs on our willingness to follow the recipe of using mind and spirit together. Think slowly about who knows (and how) whether this recipe works or not. People who do not know from their own experience that this recipe works may assume that others also do not know by the power of the Holy Ghost, but they do not know that. Who knows better whether it is possible to make a soufflé—a chef who has made many, or someone who has not, and who does not believe it can be done, who does not really intend to make a soufflé, or who only makes insincere efforts?

I have met and read about many people who lost faith in the Restoration after feeling disillusioned. I understand that choice. A metacognitive person realizes, however, that they and everyone else choose to exercise faith in something. Everyone exercises faith in things they cannot see and do not *know* in the same sense that they know with their senses. Atheists do not *know* there is no God. Rather, they choose to believe without proof that verifiable facts are best interpreted to mean that there is no God. Studies indicate that about half of the scientists in America believe in some sort of deity or higher power. That remained steady for more than a century.[3] That verifiable fact can be interpreted to mean that science reveals some kinds of knowledge, but not whether God exists. Starting from the same set of scientific facts, about half of the scientists put faith in the idea that there is no God while the other half put faith in the idea that there is.[4] We sometimes want to cope with the uncertainties of life with the cognitive illusion that we choose reason *instead* of faith. But everyone chooses to have faith in something, including in reason. The Restoration declares that the sure place to put one's faith is *in Jesus Christ*. Many, many people who have done that testify that their faith has been surely placed.

I testify from repeated personal experience that the Restoration's recipe works. When we combine the brain work of thinking slowly with the spiritual work of exercising faith in Jesus Christ, having a sincere heart and real intent, and asking God to reveal to us, we can know the truth about "matters that involve eternal consequences."[5] When that happens, we may know less than we thought we did before. But we *know* what Joseph knew the way Joseph knew. So think slowly and do spiritual work. Then you will know how you know what you know.

2.

What Kind of a Being Is God?

Professor Stephen H. Webb (1961–2016) was a devout and learned disciple of the Savior. He was not a Latter-day Saint, but he wrote the book *Mormon Christianity: What Other Christians Can Learn from the Latter-day Saints*. It says:

> The traditional view, which is often called classical theism, holds that God is utterly unique. God is not one of the things of this world. He is absolutely transcendent, and as such, God is utterly beyond the stretch of our imagination, let alone the range of our knowledge. We can know God only if and when God reveals himself to us, but even then we do not know God's substance (or essence). . . . Classical theists think the idea that God is embodied is nonsensical. It is like saying squares are round. If it is the nature of God to be pure spirit, then by definition God cannot have or be a body. Classical theism was slow to develop in the church [Christianity] and did not receive its most systematic treatment until the work

of Thomas Aquinas (1225–1274), but most Christians today share its *assumption* that God is immaterial.[1]

According to Professor Webb, Christians generally assume—but do not know—that God is immaterial. One of the most important elements of thinking slowly is discerning the difference between facts and assumptions. Throughout this book, *facts* refers to things that are verifiably true regardless of what a person thinks about them.

That definition needs further qualification. I mean historical facts, or things that can be verified by historical sources of knowledge. Please do not misunderstand. On every page I will affirm what President Dallin H. Oaks described as "the principle of independent verification by revelation."[2] The ultimate way to know something is to receive that knowledge by revelation. But this paragraph is about the beginning of knowledge, not the end, informed by President Russell M. Nelson's teaching that "good inspiration is based upon good information."[3] Start right by identifying the basic facts that are the same to all informed people regardless of whether they believe in the Restoration or not. In this sense, it is a historically verifiable fact that Joseph Smith testified that he saw a vision in a grove. It is not a historically verifiable fact that Joseph did, indeed, see what he testified that he saw. That can only be verified by revelation. Similarly, classical theism is not a historically verifiable fact. It is an assumption most Christians share, though not most Latter-day Saint Christians. We could only know whether classical theism is true if God confirmed to us by revelation that it is.

Remember Professor Webb's point that it was a thousand years after Jesus's earthly ministry before classical theism's assumption that

God is immaterial obtained its hold on Christianity. Here is a high-level overview of how that happened:

- According to the Bible, Jesus Christ, the Son of God, was born of a virgin, crucified for the sins of the world, resurrected, and ascended into heaven after promising to return someday.

- That, at least, was the testimony of eyewitnesses—apostles He chose and ordained—who contributed to biographies of Jesus and a history of their acts as apostles. Because they were eyewitnesses, their knowledge was *a posteriori* knowledge, a Latin phrase that means "based on experience."

- Eyewitness accounts were compiled and recorded in the Bible (we know their testimonies because they were recorded in historical records).

- In their historical records, apostles prophesied apostasy.

- In their letters to Christians, apostles documented apostasy.

- By about AD 100, there were no more active apostles.

- Theologians replaced the apostles and theology replaced experience and eyewitnesses. Theology is typically *a priori*, a Latin phrase that describes knowledge gained from reasoning and deduction.

- Theologians reasoned and deduced based in part on teachings of Parmenides (born about 515 BC). Philosophy professor James Faulconer wrote: "As he is usually interpreted, Parmenides gave careful, rational arguments that the transcendent ultimate must not only be unchanging, it must be unmoving, indivisible, unaffected, and outside time—since each of those things implies change. . . . Parmenides's way of thinking about reality became an embedded cultural assumption. In fact, the Parmedian assumption was all the more powerful because it was unconscious. Not knowing they were making that assumption made it difficult for early Christians to avoid it."[4]

- Beginning in AD 325, Roman emperors convened councils of bishops who were theologians. Over the course of a couple of centuries, the councils agreed on written creeds that codified the nature of God and Christ.

- In this process, based on the Parmedian assumption and using words not found in scripture, theologians decided that God and Christ were of one uncreated substance. This implied that God is immutable (does not ever change in any way) and impassible (cannot experience emotion, pleasure, pain, or anything that seems human).

When your Christian friends ask if you are a Christian, the question generally assumes the validity of classical theism. It asks, in other words, if you believe in the Christ of the creeds. If that defines a Christian, then Latter-day Saints are not Christians.

The Restoration offers an alternative. It affirms with traditional Christianity that being Christian means believing that Jesus Christ, the sinless Son of God, atoned for the sins of the world, resurrected from the dead, and will come again in glory. But the Restoration says the creeds are wrong about God. It says, "the Book of Mormon is overtly Christian from end to end."[5] It says that Jesus Christ is fixing what went wrong (restoring His church). None of that would surprise most Latter-day Saints, but it might be fresh insight to learn that Jesus regards Christianity as His church, and the restored Church of Jesus Christ as means to the end of establishing Christianity. We know this from a revelation Jesus gave to Joseph

Smith at least a year before the organization of the restored Church of Jesus Christ in 1830 (to which He added *of Latter-day Saints* in 1838). In this revelation, the Lord spoke of restoring His gospel to establish His Church. Christians, He said, did not need to fear that the restored Church would undermine Christianity—just the opposite. Those who "build up churches unto themselves" were undermining Christianity (Doctrine and Covenants 10:52–56). Jesus was restoring it. The Restoration declares that Jesus called Joseph Smith and sent His original apostles to ordain him (Doctrine and Covenants 27:12).

Now imagine it is a very pleasant spring morning, April 7, 1844, in Nauvoo, Illinois. The Mississippi River is rolling along. The prairie grass and the trees are green. It smells like spring. By 10 a.m., thousands of Latter-day Saints have gathered in the open air to listen to the last general conference talk Joseph Smith will ever give to them.[6] He knows that he does not have long to live.[7] What will he say? He decides to speak in memory of "Beloved Brother King Follet," who recently died in an accident. Joseph asks the Saints to pray that he will have the Holy Ghost and that the Lord will strengthen his lungs.

The sources of our knowledge of this talk are found on The Joseph Smith Papers website. They include Wilford Woodruff's journal entry for the day—his best effort to reconstruct Joseph's sermon. "It is necessary for us to have an understanding of God at the beginning," Joseph says, according to Wilford. "If we get a good start first we can go right, but if you start wrong you may go wrong." Joseph asked, "What kind of a being is God? . . . have any of you seen or herd him or communed with him[?] . . . The scriptures inform us that this is eternal life to know the ownly wise God & Jesus Christ whome He has sent. [So] . . . if you dont know God you have not eternal life. [So] . . . find out what kind of a being God is." Joseph then testified, "God who sits in <u>yonder</u> <u>heavens</u> is a <u>man</u> <u>like</u> <u>your-selves</u> That <u>GOD</u> if you were to see him to day that holds the worlds you would see him like a man in form, like yourselves."[8]

That restored truth challenged classical theism. Joseph learned from God that the creeds were wrong (see Joseph Smith—History 1:19). So Joseph rejected the assumption on which traditional Christianity is based—that God is immaterial. The God Joseph *knew* was not a theological abstraction. Rather, He was mutable or capable of change, of becoming God. He was also passible, meaning that He not only had a body, He had passions. He could suffer. The God who revealed himself to Joseph Smith became God and was perfectly passible. Joseph taught that all people are children of God, with potential to become like Him.

A student emailed me a delightful example of slow thinking about the idea Joseph taught that God is mutable or capable of change. She wrote: "This seems to disagree with Moroni 8:18, which states, 'For I know that God is not a partial God, neither a change-able being; but he is unchangeable from all eternity to all eternity.' I am confused why Joseph said that God is mutable but Moroni said that God is an unchangeable being. I think I'm missing a key truth here, but I am unsure what it might be. If you could respond to this email with some resources I could use to learn more about this or if we could talk about it in class, I would really appreciate that."

Notice that this student avoided the fast-thinking heuristic Daniel Kahneman called WYSIATI—what you see is all there is.[9] She recognized the apparent incongruity between the scripture and Joseph's teaching, but she metacognitively rejected the assumption

11

that what she saw was all there was: "I think I am missing some key truth here." This slow-thinking student was teachable, a seeker looking for the best sources of knowledge that could reconcile the facts. The scriptures are the best source for this knowledge. So her quest continued by thinking slowly about what the scriptures say about God's immutability. She searched the scriptures, mind you, not one single verse of scripture.

She found that Mormon's point in Moroni 8 is affirmed throughout the scriptures: God is unchanging. But the point the scriptures make (and that Mormon makes in his letter to his son) is not that God never changes in any way. The point is that God is always true to His word. In that way He is unchanging. In that way He is unchangeable.

Mormon begins his letter to his son by revealing the "words of Christ," which say that "little children are whole, for they are not capable of committing sin," so they need no baptism for the remission of sins (Moroni 8:8). Therefore, the "gross error" among the Nephites—that young children need baptism—is false (Moroni 8:6). If it were true, Mormon reasons, then God would have been untrue to His word that children are all redeemed by the Atonement of Jesus Christ. And God, Mormon testifies, is always true to His word.

Other scriptures affirm this reading. Hebrews 6 (quoting Psalm 102 about how constant and consistent God is) tells about the covenant promises God made to Abraham. It says that God showed the heirs of these promises the "immutability of his counsel" by confirming it with an oath (Hebrews 6:17). Here again the emphasis is on "the unchangeable nature of Jehovah's counsel, oaths, and promises."[10] That accords with the revelation to Joseph that says the Lord makes promises "with an immutable covenant" (Doctrine and

Covenants 98:3), and the verse that says the Lord's promise is "immutable and unchangeable" in Doctrine and Covenants 104:2. All of that is characteristic of the God of Abraham: "There is nothing that the Lord thy God shall take in his heart to do but what he will do it" (Abraham 3:17). "Therefore," the Book of Mormon declares, "ye need not suppose that ye can turn the right hand of the Lord unto the left, that he may not execute judgment unto the fulfilling of the covenant which he hath made unto the House of Israel" (3 Nephi 29:9).

"Misunderstanding," according to two Bible scholars, "comes when these ideas are *interpreted* through the lens of Greek philosophy. Classical philosophers from Plato to Plotinus and Christian theologians from Augustine through Thomas Aquinas and into the modern era have all agreed that whatever is worthwhile and true is unchanging and must therefore be immaterial."[11] The incongruity is not in the verifiable facts themselves. In other words, Joseph's teaching that God became God is not inconsistent with the scriptural truth that God makes and keeps promises faithfully. The incongruity lies in the dominant *interpretation*, which is based on the assumption of classical theism.

The scriptures teach that God is immutable in that He is unchangingly true and faithful to His promises. They also testify that He changes—that He experiences jealousy and joy, fury and compassion. He lives and loves, moves, and has being. The passible, mutable God who revealed Himself to Joseph Smith accounts for these scriptural facts better than the God of classical theism does. Thinking fast about the question of whether God changes leads generally to a knee-jerk answer *no*. Thinking slowly about it starts by asking, what is meant by *change*? Then, by a lot of scriptural brain work done prayerfully, sincerely, and with faith in Jesus Christ, we recognize that, as the scriptures affirm, God makes and keeps immutable promises. And, as the scriptures affirm, God changes in other ways all the time.

Joseph taught that God, and later Christ, had become exalted, and that because of Them we could become exalted too—but not overnight. "It will take a long time after the grave," he said. Joseph taught: "You have got to learn how to make yourselves God, king and priest, by going from a small capacity to a great capacity to the resurrection of the dead, to dwelling in everlasting burnings . . . to be an heir of God & joint heir of Jesus Christ enjoying the same rise exhaltation & glory untill you arive at the station of a God."[12]

Joseph knew that he was speaking to converted Protestant Christians who might find his teachings challenging to their assumptions about God. He turned to the first verse of the Bible and showed that his teachings were grounded there, not in Greek philosophy. He taught that the verb translated as *created* in Genesis 1:1 refers to organizing both spiritual and elemental matter into divine beings with power to become exalted as God is. From his Hebrew studies and from the Book of Abraham, Joseph knew that the word translated as *God* in Genesis 1:1 is plural—Gods. Gods created. "The Gods came together & concocked the plan of making the world & the inhabitants," he said.[13] So Joseph rejected the traditional Christian—but not Biblical—doctrine that God created out of nothing, or *ex nihilo*. Wilford and the thousands of others listening must have been on the edges of their seats.

Joseph used the ring on his finger to illustrate what the Lord had revealed to him. There are two basic kinds of stuff: element and intelligence. Neither was created or made. They cannot be. They are like a ring, Joseph said, with no beginning and no end. God and people are made from this substance. God made people out of this substance but did not make the substance—which the Lord taught Joseph to equate with light, truth, life, law, glory, power, and intelligence (see Doctrine and Covenants 88; 93). In the Lord's revelations to Joseph, obtaining more of that substance is the same as obtaining *knowledge*. "The relationship we have with God places us in a situation to advance in knowledge," Joseph said.[14] God offers us intelligence on terms and conditions (the laws of God), and we can accumulate intelligence by choosing to obey God's laws (see Doctrine and Covenants 51; 88; 93; 130). Put another way, we are endowed with God's power when we keep covenants to obey His laws. As Joseph put it, "God has power to institute laws to instruct the weaker intelligences that they may be exalted with himself."

Why restoration? Because that restored knowledge was sorely needed to course correct Christianity. We will start right if we reject unfounded assumptions about the nature of God and come to know for ourselves that we belong to a heavenly family. We are here on purpose. We are children of heavenly parents, whose divine Son, Jesus Christ, was part of the plan to exalt us in their image from the very beginning—if that is what we want. President Dallin H. Oaks declared, "Our theology begins with heavenly parents. Our highest aspiration is to be like them."[15]

Professor Webb thought slowly. He identified and interrogated the assumption of classical theism on which traditional Christianity is based. He asked, "What if Joseph Smith's vision of God really does have something important to say to all Christians today? What if his insight into the materiality of the divine is what the world today most needs to hear?"[16] Those are the slow-thinking questions of a seeker with a sincere heart, real intent, and faith in Jesus Christ. The assumption about God embedded in the Christian creeds contributed to apostasy. But Joseph Smith became good at identifying and interrogating that assumption. The next chapter tells how apostasy shaped his family so they were ready for restoration.

3.

A Family Ready for Restoration

The sixteenth-century reformation of Christianity produced various theologies. Joseph Smith's ancestors embraced the theology of John Calvin (1509–1564). His ancestors started as Puritans and Pilgrims, and eventually they were Congregationalists and Presbyterians—all of whom espoused Calvin's theology—who settled in New England in the 1600s and 1700s.

A hundred years before Joseph Smith's teenage struggle to discover the truth, a teenage student at Yale in New Haven, Connecticut, struggled to discern whether his parents' Calvinism was correct. His name was Jonathan Edwards. He was "full of objections against the doctrine of God's sovereignty, in choosing whom he would to eternal life, and rejecting whom he please; leaving them eternally to perish, and be everlastingly tormented in hell." He remembered that it "used to appear like a horrible doctrine to me." His mind changed when he "apprehended the justice and reasonableness" in the doctrine that God saved or damned everyone "according to his sovereign pleasure." Then, like Joseph Smith a century later, Jonathan read a verse in the Bible that changed the course of his life, 1 Timothy 1:17: "Now unto the King eternal, immortal, invisible, the only wise God, be honour and glory forever and ever. Amen." As Jonathan reflected on those words again and again, a sense of the glory they described filled him and inclined his heart toward God.[1]

A few years later, Jonathan wrote a love note about Sarah Pierpont. It highlighted her love for God and God's manifestations to her lovely mind.[2] Sarah and Jonathan married in 1727. A dozen years later, while listening to a prayer, Sarah yearned to, "without the least misgiving of heart, call God my Father." Pondering her experience when she was alone later, Sarah sensed that "God the Father, and the Lord Jesus Christ, seemed as distinct persons, both manifesting their inconceivable loveliness, and mildness, and gentleness, and their great immutable love to me." The experience filled Sarah with peace, "compassion and love for all mankind," and deep humility.[3]

Two years later, Sarah's husband Jonathan, now a Presbyterian Reverend in his late thirties, gave what would become a famous sermon titled "Sinners in the Hands of An Angry God." It is about God's mercy. Here is a sample from it:

> The God that holds you over the Pit of Hell, much as one holds a Spider, or some loathsome Insect, over the Fire, abhors you, and is dreadfully provoked; his Wrath towards you burns like Fire; he looks upon you as worthy of nothing else, but to be cast into the Fire; he is of purer Eyes than to bear to have you in his Sight. . . . and yet 'tis nothing but his Hand that holds you from falling into the Fire ever Moment.[4]

Mercy? Yes, because Reverend Edwards accepted the Calvinist premise that people are so depraved and deserving of fiery damnation that any postponement of it manifests God's mercy.

Both Sarah and Jonathan Edwards loved God and served Him with faith in Jesus Christ, sincere hearts, and real intent. They were not Joseph's ancestors, but they represent the tensions in their culture and the ways they struggled to know God. They also show, as Terryl Givens wrote, that "long before Joseph Smith offered his first prayer, thousands and millions of people must have yearned, as Sarah did, for the assurance that God was not the severe, distant, impersonal deity of Jonathan Edwards, but the kind, loving, and very personal God that Joseph found in the Sacred Grove."[5]

By the time Joseph went into the grove, Arminianism was encroaching hard on Calvinism. The Dutch theologian Jacobus Arminius (1560–1609) started out Calvinist but changed his views. Where Calvinism teaches that God will save some people *unconditionally*, Arminianism emphasizes God's responsiveness to human will. Arminian Christians cite scriptures that show God's salvation to be *conditional*. Think of James 1:5–6 or John 3:16. Christians who espouse Arminian theology believe Christ performed an atonement ample enough to save anyone who chooses to act on God's conditions for salvation. Calvinists believe that a person *cannot* choose to resist God's grace (because then God would not be sovereign); Arminians believe a person *can* resist God's grace. In 1738, an Anglican minister in his midthirties named John Wesley was listening to a sermon in London when he felt the Holy Ghost assure him that Christ had atoned for his sins. He became a powerful Arminian preacher. After his death in 1791, Wesley's followers founded the Methodist Church.

In the 1770s, when Joseph Smith's parents were born and his grandparents were trying to figure out which church to join, Universalism gained attention. Universalism teaches that God will ultimately save everyone. Calvinism is based on a particular reading of Paul's teachings, and Universalism is based on a particular reading of John's teachings: God is love. Why would a loving God, with power to save people, damn anyone? Universalism and Calvinism may seem like opposites, but they share the idea that God does all the decision making. Neither includes what the Restoration calls *agency*. In both Calvinism and Universalism, people do not choose to accept or reject God's plan of salvation through Christ. God makes all the choices.

Deism is another idea that attracted a lot of attention in the years leading up to the Restoration. Deism says that God created the universe and lets it run, but He does not reveal Himself through miraculous or supernatural ways. Reason is the revelation of Deism. Unlike the other *isms* Joseph encountered, Deism does not begin with the fallen Eve and Adam, and if there was no fall, there is no need for a redeemer. Deism is more philosophy than religion; Deism's Jesus is a moral philosopher, not a Savior.

If you feel bewildered by all the *isms* in the preceding paragraphs, let that give you a sense of what it was like to be Joseph Smith's grandparents and parents. All of these ideas and others competed with each other, creating confusion, uncertainty, conflict, instability, anxiety, and fear in Joseph Smith's family history. Between the dates when, and places where, Joseph's parents were born, there was a shot heard round the world that sparked the American Revolution. Political and spiritual doctrines of self-determination swept America at the same time. People who lived through that were anxious and unsettled, much as people are in our uncertain times.

By the time Lucy Mack gave birth to Joseph twenty-five years later, a Second Great Awakening had many people asking anew what, if anything, they could do to obtain salvation in Christ. By the time Joseph went into the grove, Methodism was the largest church in the United States. Imagine what it was like for a young married couple (Joseph Smith's parents-to-be) to experience all the change and tumult that turned their lives upside down in their first thirty years.

Before she was Joseph's mother, Lucy Mack was the daughter of Lydia Gates, a Calvinist, and Solomon Mack, a man without faith, though he converted to Christ later in life. Lucy married Joseph Smith in 1796. He too had parents whose religious views had changed dramatically. His parents, Mary Duty and Asael Smith, belonged to a church founded on Calvinist teachings, but his father, at least, turned to Universalism and sometimes advocated Deism too. Joseph Smith Sr. learned from his parents to love God, pray earnestly, be pious, and have contempt for self-righteousness. They also emphasized the combination of "scripture and sound reason" as the way to truth, that God does not play favorites, and that Jesus Christ "can as well save all as any."[6]

For all that, Lucy and Joseph had no church. They had Calvinism and Universalism and Deism in their blood and Arminianism all around. Each of those *isms* contended for their attention and their souls, but they did not wholeheartedly embrace any of them. They were, in fact, the first members of their families for several generations to not belong somewhere.

They worried about how they would support their growing family and what they should tell the children when they asked if they needed to be saved, and if so, how. Lucy and Joseph were Christian. They believed that the answers to their questions should center on Jesus Christ, but whose Christ? Which *ism* would they teach the children? Lucy and Joseph Sr. did not always agree on that—not with their parents, with each other, or even within themselves:

LUCY	JOSEPH SR.
• feared dying before conversion	• dreamed anxious dreams
• promised God she'd seek His Church and tried several options	• was disgusted with "formalist" clergy—those who had a form of godliness but denied God's power (2 Timothy 3:5; JS—H 1:19)
• believed that some church is better than no church	• believed that no church is better than the wrong church

In 1844–1845, Lucy wrote an important memoir. It is the source of most of our knowledge about her and her husband. In it, she told of their disagreement about her desire to explore Methodism. She pled with her husband to attend Methodist meetings with her. He did until his father berated them for it. Joseph asked Lucy to stop attending, and she was "very much hurt" that he preferred to side with his father more than her. She had long since promised God that she would search for His church until she found it. So she visited "a grove of handsome wild cherry trees and prayed" that God would incline her husband to join her quest. Lucy went home depressed, but that night she received a revelation. She dreamed vividly that her husband "would hear the pure gospel, receive it with his whole heart, and rejoice therein."[7]

Apostasy contributed to complex theological problems and confusing alternatives that fostered anxiety and uncertainty. That inclined

Joseph Smith's parents to seek for divine answers and readied them for the Restoration. Among the revelators who experienced manifestations of God's love and assurance that restoration was on the way were women including Sarah Pierpont Edwards and Lucy Mack Smith. Lucy's son Joseph learned that he, like his mother, could successfully seek God. The next chapter tells how a dilemma between Joseph's head and heart helped get the Restoration underway.

DILEMMAS

4.

Joseph's Head and
Heart Dilemma

What was it about Methodism that made Joseph "somewhat partial to it" and "desire to be united" with Methodists prior to his vision? (Joseph Smith—History 1:8). What did he mean post-vision when he told his mother, "I have learned for myself that Presbyterianism is not true"? (Joseph Smith—History 1:20). We may need a little larger sample size of both Presbyterianism and Methodism in order to understand Joseph.

As noted in the previous chapter, the most important attribute of the Presbyterian God is His absolute and complete sovereignty. He is in control. He might decide to save souls but is much more likely to damn them, and there is nothing that anyone can do about it. Reverend Edwards characterized God's sovereign will as "arbitrary" and said that He abhors us.

Methodists emphasized that people could choose to come to Christ and receive a gift of His grace that would cause them to be spiritually reborn. When that happened, converts felt pure joy. Many of them shouted for joy.

The contrast between these two theologies meant a lot to Joseph. His dilemma of not knowing which, if either of them, was right is the conflict at the heart of his vision accounts, which tell how he tried unsuccessfully to discern which was right before he successfully asked God in the grove.

In 1832, Joseph wrote a brief autobiography that is a very important source of our knowledge by and about him. It includes this passage about his early teens:

> At about the age of twelve years my mind become seriously imprest with regard to the all important concerns of for the well fare of my immortal Soul which led me to searching the scriptures believeing as I was taught, that they contained the word of God thus applying myself to them and my intimate acquaintance with those of differant denominations led me to marvel excedingly for I discovered that <they did not adorn> instead of adorning their profession by a holy walk and Godly conversation agreeable to what I found contained in that sacred depository this was a grief to my Soul thus from the age of twelve years to fifteen I pondered many things in my heart concerning the sittuation of the world of mankind the contentions and divi[si]ons the wicke[d]ness and abominations and the darkness which pervaded the of the minds of mankind my mind become excedingly distressed for I become convicted of my sins.[1]

That is how people talked in Joseph's day—*convicted of my sins.* They learned that language from the preachers. It went at least as far back as the Great Awakening encouraged by Presbyterian Reverend Edwards and continued into a Second Great Awakening during Joseph's early years, a movement that had many people asking anew what, if anything, they could do to obtain salvation in Christ. Every theology Joseph encountered gave him a different answer to that eternally consequential question.

Joseph knew he was sinful. He also knew he had not been able to do anything about that. That is what the Presbyterian option taught him to expect, so it made sense in Joseph's head. But the Methodist option appealed to Joseph's heart. He attended Methodist meetings and longed for the conversion that sinful souls experienced there. Methodism taught Joseph to expect God's grace if he wanted it. And he desperately wanted it. He later described to some friends how anxiously "He wanted to get Religion too wanted to feel & shout like the Rest but could feel nothing."[2] So no matter how much his heart wanted Methodism, it seemed to his head like the Presbyterian explanation fit the evidence best.

Joseph's heart and mind were at odds. The welfare of his immortal soul depended on knowing how to act relative to Christ's Atonement—and how to act he did not know. No matter how much brain power he put into it, he did not know if his thoughts were right, and no matter how much he tried to follow his heart, he did not know if it was leading him right. How could he know? It was a terrible problem. Two passages of Joseph's Manuscript History Book A-1, excerpted in the Pearl of Great Price as Joseph Smith—History, verses 10 and 18, highlight Joseph's dilemma:

> 10. In the midst of this war of words and tumult of opinions, I often said to myself: What is to be done? Who of all

these parties are right; or, are they all wrong together? If any one of them be right, which is it, and how shall I know it? . . . .

18. My object in going to inquire of the Lord was to know which of all the sects was right, that I might know which to join. No sooner, therefore, did I get possession of myself, so as to be able to speak, than I asked the Personages who stood above me in the light, which of all the sects was right (for at this time it had never entered into my heart that all were wrong)—and which I should join.

If we think too fast, we could conclude that those verses contradict each other, but not when we understand Joseph's dilemma. Verse 10 is about Joseph's thought process, about what happened in his *head*. He often wondered whether all the options were wrong and how he could decide. The parenthetical clause in verse 18 is about which thoughts Joseph was willing to let into his *heart*. He often considered that all avenues claiming to lead to forgiveness were dead ends. But he kept that awful thought from entering into his heart. He thought often about the possibility that maybe there was no church in which he could experience God's grace, but he was determined to seek diligently so as not to conclude that his recurring thought was true without confirmation from God. When we think slowly about these two verses, we can see how well Joseph thought slowly about his dilemma, which enabled him to exercise faith and not give up on God prematurely.

Now try to imagine what it was like to be Joseph. He knew he needed Jesus Christ. He did not know whether (the Presbyterian) God had already damned him to eternal hell by His arbitrary sovereign will, but his teenage sinfulness led him to *think* it was probably true. Joseph attended Methodist meetings where he was exhorted to be born again. Everyone around him seemed to be feeling the power of God. Joseph's family tradition told him that the scriptures *and* sound reason led to truth, but he could not resolve the conflict between his head and his heart. Only God could. After the epiphany that resulted from reading James 1:5, Joseph realized that he could ask God, and he made an early morning trip to the woods to ask in faith. When the powers of sin assailing filled his soul with deep despair, Joseph sought the God of love. His humble prayer was answered. He found the living, loving God.[3] So can you.

There is so much at stake in the sources saying that Joseph Smith saw God and Christ. Truth seekers want to learn what these sources say and simultaneously seek the revelation required to know whether what they say is true. So in the next chapter we will learn what those sources are, where they are, who made them, and why it matters.

5.

First Vision Accounts

Joseph recorded his testimony of his First Vision often. As we might expect with so much at stake, Joseph's documents are battlegrounds. Their claims are questioned and contested as well as affirmed. Seekers have an irresistible need to know these documents for themselves. They must know when and why they were created, how and by whom, and what they say. This chapter provides orientation to that, beginning with a little backstory.

In 1969, the periodical *BYU Studies* published a special issue focused on Joseph Smith's First Vision. It was in response to a potent argument published in 1967 by the Presbyterian minister Wesley Walters. The Spring 1969 issue of *BYU Studies* included articles by Professors James Allen and Milton Backman, founding fathers of scholarly First Vision studies. It included Dean Jessee's edition of two accounts of the vision (1832 and 1835) that had only recently been rediscovered in the Church's archives.

In 1970, the April issue of the Church magazine *Improvement*

Era featured Professor Allen's sophisticated but accessible article, "Eight Contemporary Accounts of Joseph Smith's First Vision: What Do We Learn from Them?" The article made a decade of recent research accessible to lay Latter-day Saints without dumbing it down. It is still a remarkable piece of historical scholarship.

In 1971, Professor Backman published the first scholarly book on the First Vision. It included all of the known vision accounts and rich context for them, including his research of the unusual religious activity in Joseph's region.

What we now know as a result of all this research is that there are four currently known primary accounts of Joseph's First Vision—written by Joseph and/or a scribe during his lifetime. There is so much at stake in them. If what they say happened actually happened—or if it didn't happen—the implications are immense. So we must investigate, interrogate, and internalize the accounts of Joseph's First Vision. And we must seek and receive revelation to tell us whether what they say happened actually happened. I started that quest thirty years ago and I have no intention of stopping. Every semester I encourage all my students to join that quest until they can answer *What do you know about Joseph Smith's first vision?* with a thorough, accurate understanding of all available sources of knowledge. I encourage them to stay on the quest until they can answer *How do you know it?* with a conviction grounded as deeply in historical sources as it is in personal revelation from God directly to them. I extend those invitations to you. As you embark, try to identify and suspend any assumptions you have about how well you already know the First Vision. Start fresh. Pray in faith for the power to hear what Joseph meant to say and to know whether he told the truth.

As we quest for truth, we should resist the temptation to think we are defective when we cannot say *I know* with a clear conscience. Everyone starts with faith in something. We can choose to put our faith in Jesus Christ. Some people have the gift "to know that Jesus Christ is the Son of God, and that he was crucified for the sins of the world." But remember that "to others it is given to believe on their words, that they also might have eternal life" (Doctrine and Covenants 46:13–14). The Restoration's *first* principle is not knowing Jesus Christ—it is choosing to put one's faith in Jesus Christ. Those who persist in that principle come to know Jesus Christ. He reveals himself to them "in his own time, and in his own way, and according to his own will" (Doctrine and Covenants 88:68).

Just as we should not "pretend to faith [we] do not have," we should not pretend to have less. "Sometimes," President Jeffrey R. Holland taught, "we act as if an honest declaration of doubt is a higher manifestation of moral courage than is an honest declaration of faith. It is not!" President Holland helped us see that hyperfocus on "the size of your faith or the degree of your knowledge" misses the mark. The variable we can choose to control "is the integrity you demonstrate toward the faith you do have and the truth you already know."[1]

To facilitate our quest to grow in faith and knowledge, this chapter will relay historically verifiable facts about these sources of knowledge, but it will not interpret the sources. Start the quest with the raw sources of knowledge and the minimal number of mediators between you and God. You only need the Lord and Joseph Smith at this point. That is because there are no historical sources of knowledge of Joseph's vision that are not mediated by Joseph. Learn from Joseph directly—not me or anyone else—what he said about seeing a vision. Then learn from God directly—not me or anyone else—whether He appeared to Joseph.

The Joseph Smith Papers has published images of all the historical sources and transcriptions of them. Googling "First Vision Accounts" will likely first lead you to these documents at ChurchofJesusChrist.org, and that site or the internet search will lead you to "Accounts of Joseph Smith's First Vision" at josephsmith papers.org. They are also accessible in the Gospel Library App. Find them there in Church History and look for First Vision. Once you get to a list of the accounts, begin with the earliest historical source, or what is now called "Joseph's History, circa Summer 1832," meaning that it was composed, as best we can tell, sometime in the summer or fall of 1832. Turn next to the November 8, 1835, entry in Joseph Smith's journal. Then read the source with which you are likely the most familiar, Joseph's Manuscript History Book A-1, excerpted as Joseph Smith—History in the Pearl of Great Price. Read the various versions of this text that were created under Joseph's direction. Then discover Joseph's 1842 letter to newspaper editor John Wentworth. After that, you will be ready to read the five known secondary accounts of Joseph's vision that were recorded by people who heard him tell it. These are available in the same places as the primary accounts. They include:

- Orson Pratt, *A[n] Interesting Account,* pages 3–5. This is the earliest published account of Joseph Smith's first vision of Deity. It was written by Orson Pratt of the Quorum of the Twelve Apostles and published as a pamphlet in Scotland in 1840.

- Orson Hyde, *Ein Ruf aus der Wüste* [A cry out of the wilderness], pages 14–16. Another member of the Quorum of the Twelve, Orson Hyde, published this account of Joseph Smith's earliest visions in Frankfurt, Germany, in 1842. He wrote the text in English, relying heavily on Pratt's *A[n] Interesting Account,* and translated it into German for publication.

- Levi Richards, Journal, 11 June 1843. Following a June 11, 1843, public church meeting at which Joseph Smith spoke of his earliest vision, Levi Richards included an account of it in his diary.

- David Nye White, "The Prairies, Joe Smith, the Temple, the Mormons, &c.," *Pittsburgh Weekly Gazette*, 15 September 1843. In August 1843, David Nye White, editor of the *Pittsburgh Weekly Gazette,* interviewed Joseph Smith in his home as part of a two-day stop in Nauvoo, Illinois. His news article included an account of Joseph Smith's First Vision.

- Alexander Neibaur, Journal, 24 May 1844. On May 24, 1844, German immigrant and Church member Alexander Neibaur visited Joseph Smith in his home and heard him relate the circumstances of his earliest visionary experience.

Those are the primary and secondary sources of knowledge about Joseph Smith's First Vision. On one hand, they document Joseph's vision well. On the other hand, they reveal little about the vision, which Joseph said defied description. Think slowly about these sources. Educate your expectations about them. Practice letting Joseph tell you what he experienced. Be metacognitive enough to identify and question any assumptions you make about what could or could not, would or would not, should or should not, have happened to Joseph. Double- and triple-check everything you know (or think you know) about the First Vision. And think about how you know what you know.

As you think, remember that not all questions are equally useful to seekers. Biased questions lead to biased answers. David Hackett Fischer is an outstanding historian who has won a Pulitzer Prize and other awards for his work. In his book *Historians' Fallacies*, Fischer says that the best questions "have an open end, which will allow a free and honest choice, with minimal bias and maximal flexibility."[2] Declarative questions violate this rule. They think too fast. They reveal bias.

Here is a declarative question about Joseph Smith's First Vision: "When Smith fails to mention foundational visions until years after the event and gives conflicting and anachronistic accounts of them, how certain can one be that he relates events as he experienced them at the time?"[3]

This inquirer thinks too fast. They assume that what they see is all there is. For example, the statement assumes that Joseph Smith failed to mention his vision for years, but no one knows for sure what Joseph said about his vision and when. All we know is that the historical records available to us say that he told a minister of the vision a few days after it, and that he could not find anyone who believed him. To say Joseph failed to mention the vision for years assumes knowledge that does not exist. Knowing that we have an account of the vision, written in Joseph's hand, dating to 1832, is not the same as knowing that Joseph did not say or write or dictate anything about the vision prior to that. And the word *fails* reveals bias.

The claim that Joseph's vision accounts are conflicting and anachronistic (out of historical order) is not a fact. It is an interpretation of verifiable facts. All scholars of Joseph's First Vision know the same verifiable facts and they disagree about whether the accounts are conflicting and anachronistic.[4] What determines this difference is not simply faith in the Restoration or lack thereof, because Stephen Prothero, a highly regarded, non-LDS religion scholar answered the question this way: "Critics of Mormonism have delighted in the discrepancies between this canonical account and earlier renditions, especially one written in Smith's own hand in 1832. . . . Such complaints, however, are much ado about relatively nothing. Any good lawyer (or historian) would expect to find contradictions in competing narratives written down years apart and decades after the event. And despite the contradictions, key elements abide."[5]

So think about the questions you and others ask. Seeking questions are open-ended, free, and honest. They have minimal bias and maximum flexibility.

We can know everything the First Vision accounts say and still not know whether Joseph saw a vision in the woods of western New York. Knowing Joseph Smith's testimony comes from historical research. Knowing that his testimony is true requires revelation, for which, thankfully, we can ask of God in faith (see James 1:5–6). We can only come to know for sure whether Joseph testified truly by following his successful way of seeking knowledge. It may not work if we are less tenacious than he was. Intellectual or spiritual laziness will hedge the way. So will any motivation other than sincere desire to know the truth. The restored way to know is not to "just pray about it." It is to read, remember, ponder, and repent, all with a sincere heart, faith in Jesus Christ, and real intent. Those who do that work come to know by the power of the Holy Ghost. They know what they know. They know how they know. Like Joseph, they can say, "I knew it, and I knew that God knew it, and I could not deny it" (Joseph Smith—History 1:25).

6.

Joseph's Other Dilemma

Besides the dilemma between heart and mind that led Joseph to seek and receive his First Vision, he had another dilemma. It may have kept him from writing about his First Vision for a long time. And it shaped the way he told it when he finally decided to do so.

Joseph Smith was in his mid-twenties, hundreds of miles from home, and anxious about his family and his soul. He was in Greenville, Indiana, nursing Newel Whitney, whose leg had been badly broken in a stagecoach accident. As Newel convalesced, Joseph went nearly every day to a grove just outside of town where he could be alone to vent his feelings in prayer. He remembered his past. He recalled his sins. He mourned and wept that he had let "the adversary of my soul . . . have so much power over me." He remembered that "God is merciful," and rejoiced that he had been forgiven and received the Comforter.

We know this because Joseph wrote it all to Emma, his wife of more than five years who was having her own ordeal trying to find a home for herself and daughter, Julia, in Kirtland, Ohio. The letter is in Joseph's hand. It is composed of just two sentences. Their average length is about 300 words. In them, Joseph jumped from topic to topic. He was a jumble of emotions. He spelled creatively. He asked Emma to excuse "my inability in convaying my ideas in writing."[1]

The inability to convey his ideas in writing was one of the horns of Joseph's dilemma. The other horn was the Lord's command to Joseph to convey his ideas in writing. The Lord had told him to keep a record, and in it, to tell the world of his calling as a seer, a translator, a prophet, and an apostle of Jesus Christ (see Doctrine and Covenants 21). Joseph had translated the Book of Mormon. Oliver Cowdery had written it. Joseph had recorded dozens of revelation manuscripts, mainly in the voice of Jesus Christ, and mostly dictated by Joseph as someone else wrote. These documents testified indeed that he was a seer, a translator, a prophet, an apostle. But none of them told the story of his first revelation. There was no known record of Joseph's vision in June 1832 when he wrote to Emma.

Joseph had no problem preaching the Book of Mormon. Moreover, he was planning to publish 10,000 copies of the Lord's revelations to him. His First Vision was different, however. It was one thing for Joseph to pray about his conflicted thoughts and deep feelings in the woods, out of sight and earshot. That, he had learned, was safe. God was forgiving and upbraided not. However, the first time Joseph told his vision (and the last until 1832, so far as we know), a minister upbraided him plenty. "Telling the story," Joseph eventually explained, "had excited a great deal of prejudice against me among professors of religion and was the cause of great persecution."[2]

To understand why Joseph felt reluctant to tell his vision and the varied ways in which he did—eventually—tell it, we need to be aware of the two horns of Joseph's dilemma:

1. He had to tell his experience.
2. He felt he was incapable of telling it.

Joseph returned to Kirtland soon after writing to Emma, and shortly after that he and his counselor/scribe Frederick Williams recorded Joseph's First Vision, quite possibly for the first time since it occurred twelve years earlier. Frederick wrote this impressive introduction:

> A History of the life of Joseph Smith Jr. an account of his marvilous experience and of all the mighty acts which he doeth in the name of Jesus Ch[r]ist the son of the living God of whom he beareth record and also an account of the rise of the church of Christ in the eve of time according as the Lord brought forth and established by his hand.

Then Frederick listed Joseph's apostolic credentials: four impressive events in Joseph's life that readers could expect to learn about in the pages that followed. First, "the testamony from on high," or what Saints would later learn to call the First Vision. Second, "the ministering of angels," meaning Moroni's call and mentoring of Joseph beginning in 1823. Third, "the reception of the holy Priesthood by the ministering of Aangels to administer the letter of the Gospel," meaning the restoration of what saints would later call the Aaronic priesthood. Finally, "a confirmation and reception of the high priesthood after the holy order of the son of the living God."[3]

No one knows why Joseph decided to pick up the pen there and finish the thought, referring to himself in the third person, as Frederick had been doing: "the Kees of the Kingdom of God conferred upon him and the continuation of the blessings of God to him." Then Joseph dragged the pen across the page, making a line to separate the introduction from what came next. Below that line, Joseph wrote about himself in the first person, and all the confidence of the introduction vanished:

> I was born in the town of Charon in the <State> of Vermont North America on the twenty third day of December AD 1805 of goodly Parents who spared no pains to instruct<ing> me in <the> christian religion at the age of about ten years my Father Joseph Smith Seignior moved to Palmyra Ontario County in the State of New York and being in indigent circumstances were obliged to labour hard for the support of a large Family having nine chilldren and as it required their exertions of all that were able to render any assistance for the support of the Family therefore we were deprived of the bennifit of an education suffice it to say I was mearly instructtid in reading and writing and the ground <rules> of Arithmatic which const[it]uted my whole literary acquirements.

Joseph confessed and exposed his mere literary abilities on this first page of his earliest autobiography. In a single sentence of 137 words, there are misspellings, awkward phrases, misplaced modifiers, and no punctuation. It is natural to wonder why Joseph apparently waited twelve years to write an account of his vision. Discovering how burdened he felt by that task helps us appreciate the fact that he ever wrote it at all.

Joseph's earliest autobiography is not just an example of his literary limits. It also includes a raw, unfiltered, and beautiful account of one of the most marvelous and consequential events to ever occur.

James Allen was a young history professor at BYU when he learned of this document in the early 1960s. He went to the Church Administration Building to study it and was overjoyed. *This is Joseph Smith pure and simple*, Professor Allen thought, *giving his feelings as best he could remember them and writing them out by himself.* Professor Allen joyfully told me about that day. "As I read that first account of the First Vision, there was that feeling that came over me that I don't think I'd ever experienced before and not quite like anything I've experienced since. It said to me, 'This young man is telling the truth.' It was a powerful story, a handwritten story that didn't have very good grammar, nor punctuation." Professor Allen said, "That confirmed the testimony that I already had, confirmed the reality and the honesty and integrity of the story of the First Vision."

I encourage you to have your own experience reading Joseph's earliest vision account. Can you hear what he was saying, or trying to say? Do you hear literary limitations that worried Joseph? Do you hear his marvelous experience? Do you sense tension between them? Fast thinking can lead to the conclusion that Joseph said he only saw one divine being: "the <Lord> opened the heavens upon me and I saw the Lord and he spake unto me." There is a lot at stake in the way the objective facts of that line are subjectively interpreted. Did Joseph see one being or two? Did he change his story over time? Can he be trusted? Some people assume that the answers to these questions are known and obvious. Let us think slowly enough to examine all the facts and interpretations ourselves, identifying and interrogating assumptions as we go. The next chapter practices source criticism of First Vision accounts, which is another way to say that it thinks about them slowly, remembering that what is at stake in these documents is not a matter of life and death. It's more important than that.

7.

Source Criticism

We may assume we know that Joseph Smith was fourteen when he saw God and Jesus Christ in a grove. That is not the same as knowing. So was Joseph fourteen or not? He probably was. Why the qualifier? Because the sources reveal that the answer is not simple or certain. The accounts say that Joseph began worrying about his soul when he was about twelve. He continued to do so through his early teens. His memory of his age at the time of his vision was vague. Joseph usually remembered his age imprecisely, and as an afterthought.

Joseph's 1832 autobiography says, "At about the age of twelve years my mind become seriously imprest with regard to the all important concerns for the well fare of my immortal Soul."[1] That led Joseph to search the scriptures and observe churches and Christians. He concluded that the scriptures and the versions of Christianity did not match. Joseph felt grief as a result. In 1832, he remembered that this process lasted "from the age of twelve to fifteen."

In 1832, Joseph did not specify his age at the time of his vision. He said simply that "while in the attitude of calling upon the Lord a piller of light above the brightness of the sun at noon day come down from above and rested upon me and I saw the Lord and he spake unto me saying Joseph my son thy sins are forgiven thee." Frederick Williams later inserted the words "in the 16th year of my age" into the clause quoted above. No one knows whether Joseph told Frederick to do so or why he wrote "16th year." Some people may think they know. That is not the same as knowing.

Joseph's scribe recorded an 1835 telling of the vision in Joseph's journal. In that telling, the last thing Joseph says about the vision is, "I was about 14 years old when I received this first communication."[2] On that day at least, his age at the time of the vision was an afterthought, and he approximated it. That line contrasts with the intense and emotional lines before it. The foreground in this memory is of Joseph discovering the truth, overcoming the unseen power that startled him, praying, seeing divine beings, and being filled with joy. His age at the time is background. It was important enough to him to try to recall at the end but not more important than that.

In his manuscript history (1838/39), Joseph remembered that unusual religious excitement started "in my fifteenth year." He was, in other words, fourteen. Of all the accounts, this one does the best job of establishing a date and situating Joseph in time: early spring, 1820. Compared to the others, this memory is uncharacteristically sharp about Joseph's age and the date of the vision. Joseph remembered later in this account, "I was an obscure boy only between fourteen and fifteen years of age," after which his scribe added, "or thereabouts." A later revision of this document is more typical. In it Joseph says he was "about 15 years old" during the "unusual religious excitement." Estimating like that is typical of the way Joseph dated things in his vision memories. In his letter to John Wentworth, for example, Joseph said, "When about fourteen years of age I began to reflect upon the importance of being prepared for a future state."[3]

The secondary accounts follow this pattern. Orson Pratt's says, "When somewhere about fourteen or fifteen years old, he began seriously to reflect upon the necessity of being prepared for a future state."[4] Orson Hyde's version is less wordy but no more precise: "When he had reached his fifteenth year, he began to think seriously . . . "[5] The journal of Levi Richards just says "when he was a youth he began to think about these things."[6] David Nye White quoted Joseph saying God "revealed himself to me first when I was about fourteen years old, a mere boy."[7] Alexander Neibaur's journal entry doesn't say anything about Joseph's age at the time.

Those are the facts of the historical record. That is the evidence we have on which to base an answer to the question with which we began: How old was Joseph Smith at his First Vision? If we think too fast, we may not discern the difference between what each account says and what it means. Some people interpret the vagueness and variety in Joseph's accounts as evidence that he did not see the Father or the Son. Some people think he could not possibly misremember his age if he actually saw a vision. That is not the same as knowing.

What we can know is that Joseph did not remember exactly how old he was at the time of his vision. He did not claim to. He claimed to see the Father and the Son. He knew that God knew it. He could not deny it. Like Paul, "Some said he was dishonest, others said he was mad; and he was ridiculed and reviled. But . . . he had seen a vision, he knew he had, and all the persecution under heaven could not make it otherwise" (Joseph Smith—History 1:24).

That was low stakes source criticism, a good warm-up. But there is a bigger question to which we now turn: Did Joseph Smith see one divine being or two in his First Vision? The question may seem absurd to anyone who knows the line from his canonized account:

> I saw two personages (whose brightness and glory defy all description) standing above me in the air. One of <them> spake unto me calling me by name and said (pointing to the other) "This is my beloved Son, Hear him."[8]

But several years before those words were written by his scribe, Joseph penned in his own hand, "the <Lord> opened the heavens upon me and I saw the Lord."[9] The distinction between the 1832 account's apparent reference to only one being—the Lord—and the Manuscript History's unequivocal assertion of two beings has led some to wonder and others to criticize Joseph for changing his story. But it may be that we just need to slow down and listen more carefully to Joseph tell the story. When we do that, we can hear him explaining that he saw at least two divine beings in the woods but not necessarily simultaneously. In 1832 he wrote, "the <Lord> opened the heavens upon me and I saw the Lord."[10] His 1839 account says clearly, "I saw two personages"[11] and the 1842 account adds, "two glorious personages."[12]

Joseph's 1835 account provides the clearest chronology. He said:

> A pillar of fire appeared above my head, it presently rested down upon me, and filled me with Joy unspeakable, a personage appeard in the midst of this pillar of flame which was spread all around, and yet nothing consumed, another personage soon appeard like unto the first, he said unto me thy sins are forgiven thee.[13]

Two of the five secondary accounts also say that Joseph first saw one divine personage who then revealed the other. In an 1843 newspaper interview, Joseph reportedly said: "I saw a light, and then a glorious personage in the light, and then another personage, and the first personage said to the second, 'Behold my beloved Son, hear him.'"[14] In 1844, Joseph told Alexander Neibaur that he "saw a personage in the fire . . . after a w[h]ile a other person came to the side of the first."[15] In the 1835 account Joseph also added as an afterthought, "and I saw many angels in this vision."[16]

Nothing in any of the accounts requires us to read these variations as exclusive of each other. In other words, there is no reason to suppose that when Joseph says, "I saw two personages," he means that he saw them at exactly the same time for precisely the same length of time, or that he did not also see others besides the two. We may assume that is what he meant. That is not the same thing as knowing what he meant. So how can we know what he meant? Because the 1835 account and two of the secondary statements assert that Joseph saw one being who then revealed the other, we should consider that he may have been trying to express that in 1832 as well. Maybe he tried to explain as best he then could that he saw one being who then revealed another, referring to both beings as "the Lord": "the <Lord> opened the heavens upon me and I saw the Lord."

Notice that the first instance of the word *Lord* was inserted into the sentence after the original flow of words, as if Joseph did not know quite how to identify the Being. Or he may have written, "I was filled with the spirit of god and he opened the heavens upon me and I saw the Lord," and then tried to improve it by adding a *t* in front of *he* to make *the*, which would create the need to insert *Lord* after the fact.

We should also consider the possibility that Joseph evoked Psalm 110, which, in the King James Bible, refers to two different divine beings both as Lord: "The Lord said unto my Lord, Sit thou at my right hand, until I make thine enemies thy footstool" (Psalm 110:1). John Welch and James Allen noticed that echo. Observing that Jesus himself evoked that verse according to Mark 12:26, they concluded that "if David could use the word 'Lord' in Psalm 110:1 . . . to refer first to the Father and then to the Son (see Mark 12:36), so could Joseph."[17] We cannot be sure about this interpretation simply from source criticism, but we cannot rule it out either.

In 1842, Joseph said that he "saw two glorious personages who exactly resembled each other in features, and likeness."[18] So four out of nine accounts of his vision say he saw two personages, three accounts say he saw one who then revealed another, and, as we have seen, the 1832 account may imply that. Only one of the nine, the Levi Richards journal entry, does not specify. It says:

> when he was a youth he began to think about these these
> things but could not find out which of all the sects were
> right— he went into the grove & enquired of the Lord which
> of all the sects were right— re received for answer that none
> of them were right, that they were all wrong, & that the
> Everlasting covena[n]t was broken.[19]

Next time someone declares that Joseph Smith said he only saw one divine being in 1832, ask how they know. Some who make that claim have studied the evidence; others are simply parroting what they have heard. Hearsay is only knowledge that you heard a claim.

It is not knowledge that what you heard is true. What if the claim you heard is partial, meaning both incomplete and biased? Why rely on the hearsay of someone who does not know what they claim to know or how they know it?

I know what all the First Vision accounts say, when they were composed, how, by whom, and in what context and circumstances. And I do not know whether Joseph meant in 1832 to refer to one divine being or two. In light of all the evidence, it seems presumptuous to conclude that there is no other choice but that he must have only meant one. We should be aware of the biases that inform our interpretation. One biased reason to choose to interpret the facts to mean that Joseph claimed to see only one divine being is that it leads to the conclusion that he changed his story because it is not true. I consciously choose to interpret Joseph differently—trustingly. I believe that the preponderance of all the evidence is best explained by the interpretation that Joseph struggled against his literary limits to tell, over time, a vision he actually experienced but that defied all description.

So did Joseph Smith see one divine being or two in his First Vision? Well, seven times out of nine he said he saw two. One time the recorder did not capture enough of his account for us to know. And one time he wrote, "the <Lord> opened the heavens upon me and I saw the Lord." Those are the verifiable facts. How we interpret them reveals more about what we want to believe about God than it does about Joseph or the sources of his vision.

PROBLEMS

8.

A Teenage Seer

Joseph's 1832 history of his life includes several cycles of the same story. In each cycle, Joseph tells about a problem he has. Then he tells how he tried to solve it and failed. After that, he tells how he turned to the Lord for a solution and succeeded. Then he starts a new cycle with the next problem.

In the first cycle, Joseph's problem is sin. He searched the scriptures and became intimately acquainted with available versions of Christianity, but that did not solve his problem. Neither did flirting with atheism or Deism. Only mourning his sinful state, exercising faith in Jesus Christ, and crying to the Lord for forgiveness resolved the problem, when Joseph heard the first revealed words of the Restoration: "Joseph, my son, thy sins are forgiven thee."[1]

Joseph's autobiography transitions from the first cycle to the second like this: "My soul was filled with love and for many days I could rejoice with great Joy and the Lord was with me but could find none that would believe the hevnly vision nevertheless I pondered these things in my heart but after many days I fell into transgressions and sinned in many things which brought a wound upon my soul and . . . when I was seventeen years of age I called again upon the Lord and he shewed unto me a heavenly vision for behold an angel of the Lord came and stood before me and he called me by name and he said the Lord had forgiven me my sins."[2]

An entry in Joseph's journal written a few years later tells the story this way: "When I was about 17 years old I saw another vision of angels, in the night season after I had retired to bed I had not been a sleep, ~~when~~ but was meditating upon my past life and experiance, I was verry concious that I had not kept the commandments, and I repented hartily for all my sins and transgression, and humbled myself before Him; <whose eyes are over all things>, all at once the room was iluminated above the brightness of the sun an angel appeared before me, his hands and feet were naked pure and white, and he stood between the floors of the room, clothed <with> ~~in~~ purity inexpressible, he said unto me I am a messenger sent from God, be faithful and keep his commandments in all things, he told me of a sacred record which was written on plates of gold, I saw in the vision the place where they were deposited."[3]

Joseph's problem in the next cycle was how to obtain the plates. When he tried and failed three times the day after the angel first visited, he cried to the Lord in agony, the angel appeared again, and told Joseph he needed to repent, gain experience, and learn to obey in order to obtain the plates. Joseph learned that he was in a period of probation. "I had been tempted of the advisary and saught the Plates to obtain riches and kept not the commandment that I should have an eye single to the Glory of God," he wrote, "therefore I was chastened and saught diligently to obtain the plates," a probationary process that took four years.[4] But it did not have to take four years.

Thinking fast, we may remember that Joseph's Manuscript History says plainly that Moroni informed him that the time for obtaining the plates "had not yet arrived, neither would untill four years from that time."[5] It is easy to assume, then, that Joseph knew on his first trip to obtain the plates that it would take him four years to get them. But when we slow down and learn all the facts from the records related to this, including the fact that Joseph Smith—History was written many years after the events it describes, then we hear what Joseph meant. Verse 53 is a mix of *factual memory* (what Joseph knew at the time) and <u>interpretive memory</u> (what Joseph only knew after the passage of time):

> I made an attempt to take them out, but was forbidden by the messenger, and was again informed that the time for bringing them forth had not yet arrived, <u>neither would it, until four years from that time;</u> but he told me that I should come to that place precisely in one year from that time, and that he would there meet with me, and that I should continue to do so until the time should come for obtaining the plates. (Joseph Smith—History 1:53; emphasis added)

All Joseph knew at the time was that his choices had prevented him from obtaining the plates then, and he should return in one year and continue faithfully until the unspecified time came. Joseph was not simply to pass time until he got the plates regardless of his behavior. He was to prepare himself by gaining experience in keeping God's commands and resisting temptations; he was to prove himself faithful to the Lord's instructions and get the plates because of his obedience. According to Joseph's mother, the angel told Joseph that "he could not take them from the place wherein they were deposited, until he had learned to keep the commandments of God," clarifying that Joseph needed to become "not only willing, but able to do it."[6]

Over time, Moroni's tutelage helped Joseph become the choice seer he was prophesied to be (see 2 Nephi 3). It prepared him to translate the Book of Mormon by the gift and power of God. Understanding the cultural circumstances in which Moroni mentored Joseph enhances our understanding of Moroni's mentorship and our appreciation for Joseph's growth, preparation, gifts, and calling. Just like discerning the difference between factual and interpretive memory is the key to verse 53, knowing Joseph's cultural circumstances during his probationary period helps us hear what Joseph is saying (and not saying) in Joseph Smith—History 1:27–65.

Sometime between his First Vision and before Moroni's first visit to him, Joseph Smith discovered that he was a seer. He told a justice of the peace about it a few years later.

According to one account of that conversation, Joseph "said when he was a lad, he heard of a neighboring girl some three miles from him, who could look into a glass and see anything however hidden from others; that he was seized with a strong desire to see her and her glass; that after much effort he induced his parents to let him visit her. He did so, and was permitted to look in the glass, which was placed in a hat to exclude the light. He was greatly surprised to see but one thing, which was a small stone, a great way off. It soon became luminous, and dazzled his eyes, and after a short time it became as intense as the mid-day sun. He said that the stone was under the roots of a tree or shrub as large as his arm, situated about a mile up a small stream that puts in on the South side of Lake Erie, not far from the New York and Pennsylvania line."[7]

Joseph testified that he had gone and found the stone, washed it, dried it, and put it in his hat, "and discovered that time, place, and distance were annihilated, and that all intervening obstacles were removed, and that he possessed one of the attributes of Deity, an All Seeing Eye. He arose with a thankful heart. . . . On the request of the court he exhibited the stone. It was about the size of a small hen's egg . . . "[8]

According to The Joseph Smith Papers, "By 1825 Joseph Smith had a reputation in Manchester and Palmyra, New York, for his activities as a treasure seer, or someone who used a seer stone to locate gold or other valuable objects buried in the earth."[9] Joseph Smith lived in a world where people believed in magic and spirits and supernatural forces. That world was being eclipsed by the enlightened world, where magic and spirits were dismissed as superstition, and everything came to be explained by natural forces rather than supernatural ones.

Washington Irving (1783–1859) wrote stories about the enchanted world Joseph knew, including stories about money diggers. One of Irving's stories, published in 1824, the year after Moroni first visited Joseph, tells of a nocturnal treasure dig in which a scryer or seer with green glasses and a forked divining rod finds the location of a buried treasure, silently draws a circle around it, and performs ceremonies "to prevent the evil spirits which keep about buried treasure from doing them any harm." Then fisherman Sam dug "a considerable hole" while the scryer, "by the aid of his spectacles, read off several forms of conjuration," and Wolfert Webber "bent anxiously over the pit, watching every stroke of the spade."

"At length the spade of the fisherman struck upon something that sounded hollow. . . . ''Tis a chest,' said Sam. 'Full of gold, I'll warrant it!' cried Wolfert."

Just then they heard a sound, looked up, and saw on the rocks above them in a red cap "what appeared to be the grim visage of [a] drowned buccaneer, grinning hideously." Then the seer dropped his divining rod and ran one way, Sam "leaped out of the hole" and ran another way, while "Wolfert made for the water." Each eventually made their way home and told their tales, but "whether any treasure was ever actually buried at that place, whether, if so, it was carried off at night by those who had buried it; or whether it still remains there under the guardianship of gnomes and spirits . . . is all a matter of conjecture."[10]

There is a lot of evidence that Joseph Smith actually participated in the kinds of activities that Irving wrote fiction about. As in Irving's story, however, there is no evidence that Joseph or his peers ever found the treasures they sought. Treasure-seeking culture was real, including the gift of seeing, but the treasures were probably legendary or imaginary.

We know this in part from a variety of reliable documents that triangulate some of the claims of less reliable documents. The most reliable documents affirm that the people who knew Joseph best believed most in his gift—his divine ability to see. For example, his mother testified that Josiah Stowell came from Pennsylvania to hire Joseph, "having heard, that he was in possession of certain *means*, by which he could discern things, that could not be seen by the natural eye."[11]

Stowell testified that Joseph "possessed all the power he claimed, and declared he could see things fifty feet below the surface of the earth, as plain as the witness could see what was on the Justices' table, and described very many circumstances to confirm his words." When the justice of the peace questioned Josiah, he affirmed, "It is not a matter of belief: I positively know it to be true."[12]

Martin Harris knew it too. He said: "I was at the house of his father in Manchester, two miles south of Palmyra village, and was picking my teeth with a pin. . . . The pin caught in my teeth, and dropped from my fingers into shavings and straw. I jumped from the bars and looked for it. Joseph and Northrop Sweet also did the same. We could not find it. I then took Joseph on surprise, and said to him—I said, 'Take your stone.' I had never seen it, and did not know that he had it with him. He had it in his pocket. He took it and placed it in his hat—the old white hat—and placed his face in his hat. I watched him closely to see that he did not look one side; he reached out his hand beyond me on the right, and moved a little stick, and there I saw the pin, which he picked up and gave to me. I know he did not look out of the hat until after he had picked up the pin."[13]

These statements affirm some of the claims of the 1834 book *Mormonism Unvailed*, which includes statements from some of Joseph's New York neighbors who were with him when he discovered a seer stone and/or when he searched for treasure. What do these witnesses know? How do they know it? They avoid incriminating themselves as they tell of Joseph's adventures. In other words, some of them know what they know because they were with Joseph, just as eager as he was to find treasure. The facts they report can be accepted when they match those reported by Joseph, his mother, Brigham Young, and Joseph Knight:

- Joseph had a deserved reputation for being a seer.
- He discovered stones in which he could see things.

- He sometimes used one or more stones to search for treasure.

If we think fast about these facts, we might err in interpreting them. Some might assume that God would have prevented Joseph from treasure seeking before calling him as a prophet. Is it sound to assume that God would not call a gifted teenage treasure seer to become a gifted prophet? Has God given us evidence that he prevents future prophets from seeing in stones, or using their gifts for what Joseph later described as "foolish errors," the "weakness of youth," and "foibles of human nature," but not "great or malignant sins"? According to Joseph's own interpretation of the facts, it was these very "weaknesses and imperfections" that led him to seek God's love and forgiveness again, and God answered by sending Moroni to mentor Joseph into a choice seer (Joseph Smith—History 1:28–29).

If we share in the assumption that God would not call a gifted but immature teenage seer and mentor him to reach his potential as a choice seer, we can interrogate our assumption. How do we know it? Did we learn it from God or another reliable source of knowledge? Do we have any evidence for it, or only a fast-thinking conclusion based on the heuristic (or mental shortcut) that what we see is all there is?

When we think slowly about Joseph's teenage probation, listening to him tell his own story in light of what other eyewitnesses recorded, we can choose these informed interpretations of the facts:

- Joseph Smith was a prophesied seer (2 Nephi 3). He was a lowercase *s* seer long before he became the Lord's uppercase *S* Seer.

- Joseph, the plates, and the means for translating them were prepared by God to bring forth the Book of Mormon so that we could "rely upon the merits of Jesus Christ and be glorified through faith in his name, and that through [our] repentance [we] might be saved" (Doctrine and Covenants 3:20).
- Joseph lived in a transitional time, when the enchanted world was being eclipsed by the enlightened world.
- We can accept the verifiable facts Joseph's critics reported (with firsthand knowledge) without accepting their hostile interpretations of those facts.
- Joseph was intensely mentored through his formative later teens by an angel who taught him to forsake the mistaken parts of the enchanted and enlightened worlds and learn to use his gift for God's purposes.
- The past is a foreign country. They did things differently there. We should think slowly about it and avoid the heuristic that what we see is all there is.
- Joseph Smith repeatedly repented and gained God's forgiveness, and so can we.

Seer stones only became superstitions recently. They are attested in the Bible and other ancient sources, and in early modern sources like a drawing of John Dee's stone. Isaac Newton and other magician/mathematician/philosophers coveted stones with marvelous powers. We may not know how God works by marvelous means—that is not the same thing as knowing that He does not. Alma warned Helaman not to assume that God could not or would not or did not work by "means" including stones, and Alma quoted a prophecy from the Savior saying that he would prepare a stone for his servant, "which shall shine forth in darkness unto light" (Alma 37:23).

Brigham Young knew that Joseph Smith was a seer and how Joseph became a seer. Brigham taught that "there are thousands in the world who are natural born Seers, but when the Lord selected Joseph Smith to be his . . . mouthpiece upon the earth in this dispensation, he saw that he would be faithful and honor his calling."[14] Long ago, President Dallin H. Oaks taught, "Some sources close to Joseph Smith claim that in his youth, during his spiritual immaturity prior to his being entrusted with the Book of Mormon plates, he sometimes used a stone in seeking for treasure. Whether this is so or not, we need to remember that no prophet is free from human frailties, especially before he is called to devote his life to the Lord's work. Line upon line, young Joseph Smith expanded his faith and understanding and his spiritual gifts matured until he stood with power and stature as the Prophet of the Restoration."[15] The next chapter tells how Joseph expanded his faith and understanding and how his spiritual gifts matured.

9.

Two Problems of Book of Mormon Translation

Joseph's problems did not end when he obtained the plates. In his 1832 autobiography, he tells how God helped him obtain them, then says his next problem was not knowing how to get the writing on them translated. As usual, Joseph did his best to try to solve the problem himself. When that did not work, he tried the divinely appointed way of using stones "the Lord had prepared . . . for to read the Book."[1]

This chapter delves into what we know about the Lord's solution to Joseph's problem: how to get the Book of Mormon translated. It also highlights our problem: What do we know about Book of Mormon translation and how do we know it?

Joseph Smith did not know how to translate the writing on the plates. The historical records say that the Lord provided him with the plates and "means" or stones for translating them, but there is no evidence that Joseph knew what to do or how to do it. Apparently, the Lord let him work it out in a way that seems similar to when

Jared's brother figured out how to light his barges (see Ether 2–3), and to how Oliver Cowdery learned that translating did not occur spontaneously without intellectual and spiritual work (see Doctrine and Covenants 8–9).

So how did Joseph and his associates solve the problem of translating the Book of Mormon? Joseph's 1832 autobiography tells us a little about his early efforts at learning to translate, and how he discovered that he was part of Isaiah's prophecy that the Lord would bring forth his marvelous work:

> I was married to Emma Hale Daughtr of Isaach [Isaac] Hale who lived in Harmony Susquehan[n]a County Pensylvania on the 18th January AD, 1827, on the 22d day of Sept of this same year I obtained the plat[e]s—and in December following we mooved to Susquehana by the assistence of a man by the name of Martin Har[r]is who became convinced of th[e] vision and gave me fifty Dollars to bare my expences and because of his faith and this rightheous deed the Lord appeared unto him in a vision and shewed unto him his marvilous work which he was about to do and <h[e]> imediately came to Suquehannah and said the Lord had shown him that he must go to new York City <with> some of the characters so we proceeded to coppy some of them and he took his Journy to the Eastern Cittys and to the Learned <saying> read this I pray thee and the learned said I cannot but if he would bring the blates [plates] they would read it but the Lord had forbid it and he returned to me and gave them to <me> <to> translate and I said cannot for I am not learned but the Lord had prepared spectacles for to read the Book therefore I commenced translating the characters

and thus the Propicy [prophecy] of Isiaah was fulfilled which is writen in the 29 chaptr concerning the book.[2]

Joseph Smith consistently used the phrase from Omni 1:20—"the gift and power of God"—to describe how he translated the Book of Mormon.[3] He did not elaborate much on what that meant. In fact, when his brother asked him to, Joseph said "that it was not intended to tell the world all the particulars of the coming forth of the book of Mormon."[4]

But three kinds of evidence provide some insight:

1. Passages in the Book of Mormon that talk about "means" or instruments the Lord prepared (and seers used) for translation.
2. What remains of the original manuscript of the Book of Mormon and the backup copy we call the printer's manuscript.
3. Records of witnesses who watched and/or assisted Joseph translate.

It is well-known that the Lord touched sixteen stones for Jared's brother, but less well-known that the very next story in Ether 3 is the Lord giving him commands about what to write, and giving him two additional stones to keep with his writings so they could later be translated and read (Ether 3:21–25).

Later, when a king asked Ammon, "Canst thou translate?" Ammon said he could not, but the King in Zarahemla could because he had a "high gift from God," including "interpreters," and God's commission to see in them. Ammon (or Mormon) referred to all this as "means" whereby God brought about his ends (Mosiah 8:11–18). In Alma 37, Alma taught his son Helaman what he needed to know to become the keeper of the sacred records and the seer stones God prepared to translate them. In that process Alma used the word *means* three times in the same way it is used in Mosiah 8, to refer to divine means prepared for translating sacred text.

Latter-day Saints often cite Alma's words in Alma 37:6–7 without realizing that by "small means" Alma refers to seer stones, or what he calls interpreters. Verse 23 includes a revelation from the Lord, which Alma quotes to support his teaching that the Lord prepared small means to bring about his purposes: "And the Lord said: I will prepare unto my servant Gazelem, a stone, which shall shine forth in darkness unto light, that I may discover unto my people who serve me, that I may discover unto them the works of their brethren, yea, their secret works, their works of darkness, and their wickedness and abominations."

No one knows for sure how to read this verse; Gazelem could be a name or title of the Lord's servant (either Joseph or some other servant), or it could refer to the stone that shines forth in darkness, or both. One thing we know is that Joseph Smith identified with Gazelem. And we know that the Lord's revelations to Joseph, and Lucy Mack Smith's memoir, use the word *means* in this same way, to refer to divinely prepared stones as aids to receiving revelation.[5]

The month I turned four years old, the *Friend* magazine for children featured an article that said:

> Translating the ancient and strange looking writing on the gold plates was not a job that just anyone could do. Such an important work needed to be done by someone who was especially prepared by the Lord to do it.
>
> Because of his spiritual nature and his willingness to learn

the truth, Joseph Smith was tested and found worthy to be the translator of the Book of Mormon. To help him with the translation, Joseph found with the gold plates "a curious instrument which the ancients called Urim and Thummim, which consisted of two transparent stones set in a rim of a bow fastened to a breastplate."

Joseph also used an egg-shaped, brown rock for translating called a seer stone.[6]

I did not read that article when I was four or learn the verifiable facts it sets forth until I was in college. Ignorance of these facts contributes to our problem of not knowing what can be known about how Joseph translated the Book of Mormon. The problem is commonly compounded in at least a couple of fast-thinking ways. One is that we assume that what we see is all there is. Another is that what we think we know is often misinformation. We become complacent in what we think we know without the will or the skill to identify and interrogate our assumptions, learn the verifiable facts, and think slowly about how to interpret them in ways that best account for them.

So what are the verifiable facts of Book of Mormon translation—the ones that are the same regardless of how anyone decides to interpret them? Here are the most relevant ones:

The Book of Mormon exists. We know that. About 30 percent of the original Book of Mormon manuscript still exists. The printer's manuscript is nearly all extant. Both are almost entirely in Oliver Cowdery's handwriting. The original Book of Mormon manuscript along with the printer's manuscript show that Joseph Smith dictated, mostly to Oliver Cowdery, the text.[7] The historical record is conclusive that he did it between April 7 and the end of June 1829—less than a college semester.[8]

We know that everyone who was involved in the process said that Joseph dictated it while looking into a stone or stones, and that he did not need to have the plates in sight to do it.

Joseph Smith testified:

> With the records was found a curious instrument which the ancients called "Urim and Thummim," which consisted of two transparent stones set in the rim on a bow fastened to a breastplate. Through the medium of the Urim and Thummim I translated the record, by the gift and power of God.[9]

Emma Smith testified (to Edmund C. Briggs in 1856):

> When my husband was translating the Book of Mormon, I wrote a part of it, as he dictated each sentence, word for word, and when he came to proper names he could not pronounce, or long words, he spelled them out, and while I was writing them, if I made any mistake in spelling, he would stop me and correct my spelling, although it was impossible for him to see how I was writing them down at the time. Even the word *Sarah* he could not pronounce at first, but had to spell it, and I would pronounce it for him.
>
> When he stopped for any purpose at any time he would, when he commenced again, begin where he left off without any hesitation, and one time while he was translating he stopped suddenly, pale as a sheet, and said, "Emma, did Jerusalem have walls around it?" When I answered "Yes", he replied, "Oh! I was afraid I had been deceived." He had such

a limited knowledge of history at that time that he did not even know that Jerusalem was surrounded by walls.[10]

Martin Harris testified:

By aid of the seer stone, sentences would appear and were read by the Prophet and written by Martin, and when finished he would say, "Written," and if correctly written, that sentence would disappear and another appear in its place; but if not written correctly it remained until corrected, so that the translation was just as it was engraven on the plates, precisely in the language then used. Martin said that after continued translation they would become weary, and would go down to the river and exercise by throwing stones out on the river, etc. While doing so, on one occasion, Martin Harris found a stone very much resembling the one used for translating, and on resuming their labor of translation, he put in place the stone that he had found. He said that the Prophet remained silent, unusually and intently gazing in darkness, no traces of the usual sentences appearing. Much surprised, Joseph exclaimed, "Martin! What is the matter! All is as dark as Egypt!" Martin's countenance betrayed him, and the Prophet asked Martin why he had done so. Martin said, to stop the mouths of fools, who had told him that the Prophet had learned those sentences and was merely repeating them, etc. Martin said further that the seer stones differed in appearance entirely from the Urim and Thummim obtained with the plates which were two clear stones set in two rims, very much resembling spectacles, only they were larger. Martin said, there are not many pages translated what he wrote, after which Oliver Cowdery and others did the writing.[11]

Oliver Cowdery testified in 1834:

> Those were days never to be forgotten- to sit under the sound of a voice dictated by the inspiration of heaven, awakened the utmost gratitude of this bosom! Day after day I continued, uninterrupted, to write from his mouth, as he translated, with the Urim and Thummim, or, as the Nephites whould have said, "Interpreters," the history, or record, called "The book of Mormon". . . .[12]

In 1848, Oliver Cowdery returned to the church after a decade of disaffection. According to Reuben Miller's journal, Oliver testified:

> Friends and brethren my name is Cowdrey, Oliver Cowdrey, In the early history of this church I stood Identified with her. And [was] one in her councils. . . . I wrote with my own pen the intire book of mormon (Save a few pages) as it fell from the Lips of the prophet [Joseph Smith]. As he translated <it> by the gift and power of god, By [the] means of the urum and thummim, or as it is called by that book holy Interperters. I beheld with my eyes. And handled with my hands the gold plates from which it was translated. I also beheld the Interpreters. That book is true. Sidney Rigdon did not write it. Mr [Solomon] Spaulding did not write it. I wrote it myself as it fell from the Lips of the prophet.[13]

So according to the historical record, Joseph solved the problem of not knowing how to translate the Book of Mormon by study and by faith in the gift and power of God. The Book of Mormon tells of ancient seers and seer stones the Lord prepared to make it possible to transmit sacred records from one language to another. Joseph the seer translated the Book of Mormon by the same kind of means, given to him by the gift and power of God. Translation *of* the Book of Mormon happened the same way as translation *in* the Book of Mormon (see Omni 1:20; Mosiah 8:8–14; Mosiah 28:10–16; Alma 37; and Ether 3:22–24.)

Okay, someone might respond, but it just could not have happened the way the eyewitnesses all say it happened—Joseph dictating the Book of Mormon while looking into a stone or stones buried in his hat, not even looking at the plates. To which a seeker asks, *how do you know that?* There are many sources of firsthand knowledge affirming that Joseph produced a book between April and June 1829 in that very way.[14] What evidence is there that he did not?

One answer to that may be artistic depictions of the translation. Many well-known images do not match the historical documents from eyewitnesses and instead depict Joseph and others looking at the plates laid out on a table. So if what we think we know derives in whole or in part from sources like these, we should think more slowly about what we know and how we know it.

More recent images depict things differently. The film that plays at the Church's visitor center in Harmony, Pennsylvania, is based on careful research of the historical sources. It depicts Joseph looking into a hat while his hand rests on the cloth-covered plates.

Fast-thinkers are vulnerable to dissonance because thinking fast about Joseph's problem of how to get the Book of Mormon translated and our problem of discerning what we know about how Joseph translated and how we know it leads us to assume we know what we do not, and when our ignorance is exposed to verifiable facts, we experience dissonance—a sense of inner turmoil over seemingly irreconcilable differences.

No one likes that experience, so when it occurs, we work to reduce the dissonance to tolerable levels. That can be done by continuing to think fast. Or it can be done by slowing down, sorting verifiable facts from hearsay and misinformation, discerning the difference between facts and interpretations, quitting the practice of doing hypothetical history by assuming what would have happened *if* our hypothesis determined history, and practicing the historical method of seeking knowledge from the best sources, recognizing that what we see is not all there is, and interpreting the known facts coherently and consistently.

How can we solve the problem of knowing how Joseph translated? By seeking out of the *best* books—the Book of Mormon (including manuscripts)—the *Friend* magazine, Joseph's histories, eyewitness accounts (not paintings)—and by identifying and interrogating our assumptions. The best books all affirm that the Book of Mormon is the marvelous work and wonder Isaiah prophesied that the God of Israel would bring forth.

10.

Another Problem of Book of Mormon Translation

The fact of the Book of Mormon's existence poses another problem. Whether a person believes the Book of Mormon was revealed by God or not, it verifiably came from Grandin's Press in Palmyra, New York, in March 1830, having been typeset primarily by John Gilbert from manuscripts in Oliver Cowdery's handwriting. Those are facts that truth seekers must account for. The historical record consistently and thoroughly accounts for these facts by testifying that Joseph Smith translated the book by the power of God between April and June 1829.

Brian Hales published a longitudinal study of the other interpretations that have been given over time, including:

- Joseph Smith plagiarized a manuscript written by Solomon Spaulding.
- People besides Joseph collaborated with him.
- Mental illness enabled Joseph to write it.

- Joseph composed it by the phenomenon of automatic writing.
- Joseph wrote the book himself.[1]

Brian showed that none of the naturalistic explanations are evidence based. None of them account for the evidence well enough to obtain consensus and endure.

The most popular naturalistic theory currently is that Joseph wrote the book himself, though none of the witnesses or scribes thought so. In an interview by Joseph Smith III of his mother, Emma Hale Smith, she is reported to have given the following answers:

Q. What of the truth of Mormonism?

A. I know Mormonism to be the truth; and believe the Church to have been established by divine direction. I have complete faith in it. In writing for your father I frequently wrote day after day, often sitting at the table close by him, he sitting with his face buried in his hat, with the stone in it, and dictating hour after hour with nothing between us.

Q. Had he not a book or manuscript from which he read, or dictated to you?

A. He had neither manuscript nor book to read from.

Q. Could he not have had, and you not know it?

A. If he had had anything of the kind he could not have concealed it from me.

Q. Are you sure that he had the plates at the time you were writing for him?

A. The plates often lay on the table without any attempt at concealment, wrapped in a small linen tablecloth, which I had given him to fold them in. I once felt of the plates, as they thus lay on the table, tracing their outline and shape. They seemed to be pliable like thick paper, and would rustle with a metallic sound when the edges were moved by the thumb, as one does sometimes thumb the edges of a book.

Q. Where did father and Oliver Cowdery write?

A. Oliver Cowdery and your father wrote in the room where I was at work.

Q. Could not father have dictated the Book of Mormon to you, Oliver Cowdery and the others who wrote for him, after having first written it, or having first read it out of some book?

A. Joseph Smith [and for the first time she used his name direct, having usually used the words, "your father" or "my husband"] could neither write nor dictate a coherent and well-worded letter; let alone dictating a book like the Book of Mormon. And, though I was an active participant in the scenes that transpired, and was present during the translation of the plates, and had cognizance of things as they transpired, it is marvelous to me, "a marvel and a wonder," as much so as to anyone else.[2]

Source critics of this document note wisely that there are good reasons to think slowly about its claims and subject them to all available methods of verification. It was published a few months after Emma's death. It is not possible to know how accurately it represents her views. It includes statements that are verifiably untrue.[3] But as with *Mormonism Unvailed*, it can be triangulated with other sources. What it says about Book of Mormon translation and Joseph's literary limits is consistent with Emma's 1856 statement and with the statements of other eyewitnesses.[4]

Some posts on Reddit respond to the claim Emma reportedly made about Joseph's inability to dictate or write a coherent, well-worded letter. One of them asks, "With all the letters and documents stating the opposite of this, that he [Joseph Smith] was a good story teller and very imaginative, who are we to believe?"[5] When we think slowly about that question, we can see that it thinks too fast. It's a declarative question, meaning that it doesn't have an open end.[6] Declarative questions reveal bias. So one way to recognize our biases and educate them is to think about our questions. Notice that this one says, "With all the letters and documents stating the *opposite* of this," with *this* referring to Emma's reported claim that Joseph could not write or dictate a well-worded letter, let alone a book. The question assumes that documents saying that Joseph was an imaginative storyteller contradict the claim that he was not able to dictate or write well. But if there is evidence that Joseph was an imaginative storyteller, it does not necessarily disprove Emma's reported statement or have implications for the Book of Mormon.

Since declarative questions prejudice answers, it is better to ask seeking questions, like this: What, if any, evidence exists that Joseph was a good storyteller, or that he was imaginative? What might that evidence mean for the Book of Mormon? The best available answer comes from systematic study of all the evidence of Joseph's storytelling in light of all the witness documents, the Book of Mormon, and especially Joseph's own handwritten documents. We do not need to accept any single document or witness—we have a rich and varied collection of records that can help answer this question. We can add them all up and see what they amount to. Then we can interpret them in a way that is consistent with all the evidence, not selective pieces of it. People with a sincere heart and real intent do the work to learn what that research has revealed.[7]

Meanwhile, a short answer to the Reddit question goes like this: The most relevant and substantial document claiming that Joseph was imaginative and a storyteller is his mother's memoir, written in 1844–1845. It echoes and affirms Joseph's accounts in saying that an angel revealed the Book of Mormon plates to him and instructed him through a probationary period. Lucy adds that the family gathered each evening to listen

> in breathless anxiety to the <religious> teachings of a boy 19 years of age who had never read the Bible through by course in his life for Joseph was less inclined to the study of books than any child we had but much more given to reflection and deep study. We were convinced that God was about to bring to light something that we might stay our minds upon. . . . In the course of our evening conversations Joseph would give us some of the most amusing recitals which could be imagined. He would describe the ancient inhabitants of this continent their dress and manner of traveling the animals which they rode the cities that were built by them the structure of their buildings with every particular of their mode of warfare their religious worship as particularly as though he had spent his life with them.[8]

Lucy's memoir affirms Joseph's testimony that he brought forth the Book of Mormon by the power of God. So do all accounts of all the eyewitnesses.

The claim Emma reportedly made that Joseph could not compose a well-worded letter—whether Emma made the claim or not—can be assessed in light of Joseph's actual letters and other writings. There are two known letters by Joseph dated 1829–1830, when the Book of Mormon was translated and published, but only later copies of them are known to exist, and they are written by others.[9] Two more Joseph Smith letters dated 1831 include the earliest one we have in Joseph's own hand.[10] These are not literary masterpieces, but they are coherent. His next letter is the June 6, 1832, one analyzed earlier—beautiful, but composed of just two long sentences that demonstrate what Joseph acknowledged as "my inability in convaying my ideas in writing."[11] In a letter from Joseph that fall, written partly by him and partly by Frederick Williams, Joseph lamented that he felt locked in the "narrow prison . . . of paper pen and ink."[12] He began keeping a diary that day, making terse, disjointed entries for ten days, then not for ten months. Joseph also collaborated with Frederick Williams on a six-page autobiography around this same time.

These documents evidence that Emma's reported claim may be overstated. Joseph misplaced modifiers and made other errors, making his writing confusing. But he wrote well enough to communicate. The evidence also shows that he resisted writing, that he felt he could not compose coherent, well-worded prose, that he usually recruited help for his writing projects, and that he did not possess the literary ability to compose the Book of Mormon. So how can we account for the facts of the Book of Mormon manuscripts?

We must consider the theory that Joseph had help. After all, witnesses claim to have written for him, and the manuscripts are in their handwriting. But all of their statements affirm Joseph's testimony that he dictated the translation by the gift of God, without any other aids besides a marvelous stone or stones. So the collaboration theory is a conspiracy theory, requiring us to interpret the eyewitness evidence as intentionally falsified. To believe Joseph had help is to reject the evidence rather than accept it. Where does that lead us relative to the Reddit question about who to trust?

Trust the historical record. Everyone on record who had firsthand knowledge of the Book of Mormon translation affirms Joseph's testimony. The fact that Lucy said Joseph told his family lots of exciting things he was learning or imagining about the ancient world does not negate or undermine her witness that Joseph told the truth about the Book of Mormon. In other words, it is a false dilemma to assume that either Joseph told imaginative stories about the ancient Americas or he translated the Book of Mormon by the power of God. We could choose to interpret Lucy's account of Joseph's storytelling as completely consistent with a young man being mentored by an angel who, prior to his resurrection, was a historian as well as a religious and military leader somewhere in the Americas. If Lucy did not interpret the fact of Joseph's storytelling as evidence against the Book of Mormon, why would we? If we were unwilling to believe the Book of Mormon and needed an alternative to the historical record, it still would not account for the verifiable facts.

It is understandable, however, why some people make that choice. Those whose faith has been deeply shaken sometimes find it easier to trust lesser evidence like hearsay over the eyewitness sources. But that choice is not a foregone conclusion. It is neither inevitable nor irreversible. Rebecca Swain Williams believed the Book of Mormon and its eyewitnesses. She converted in her early thirties and wrote to share the good news with her father. He wrote back saying that she must recant. When she wouldn't, he vowed to have nothing more to do with her. She refused to let that happen, however, and persisted in loving her family, in part by praying for and sharing her testimony of the Book of Mormon with them. When family members credited false reports about contradictions between Joseph and the witnesses, Rebecca set the record straight. "I have heard the same story from several [members] of the [Smith] family and from the three witnesses themselves," she wrote, adding that she "heard them declare in public meeting that they saw an holy angel come down from heaven and brought the plates and laid them before their eyes." Rebecca knew these people well and affirmed their "good character." She believed that if her father could just know what she knew and how she knew, he too would believe. In the patriarchal blessing Rebecca received a year later, she was promised that her prayers would be answered. She kept reaching out in love and respect to her "beloved father," asked her siblings to write to her, and led her sister Sarah into The Church of Jesus Christ.[13]

Sally Bradford Parker believed the Book of Mormon and its eyewitnesses. Sally lived near Lucy Mack Smith in Kirtland and called her "one of the finest women, always helping those that stood in need. She told me the whole story. The plates were in the house and sometimes in the woods for eight months, on account of people trying to get them." Sally said that Lucy wept as she testified. When Sally asked if Lucy saw the plates, "She said no, it was not for her to see them, but she hefted and handled them and I believed all she said for I lived by her eight months and she was one of the best of women."[14]

Sally wrote this document—a letter to her sister's family—in the wake of the worst wave of disaffection The Church of Jesus Christ has ever experienced. Many Church leaders and members had changed their hearts and minds about their faith. Book of Mormon witnesses Oliver Cowdery, David Whitmer, and Martin Harris were among them—though they always affirmed their Book of Mormon testimony. In that context, Sally heard Hyrum Smith testify too: "He said he had seen the plates with his eyes and handled them with his hands." Sally explained that she was including this in the letter because of the rising "dispute [over] the Book." Worried about friends and relatives who might forsake their faith in it, she testified, "The older I grow and the more I see the stronger I feel in my mind. . . . I am as strong in the faith as when we were baptized and my mind is the same. I mean to hold on by the gospel till death."[15]

William McLellin believed the Book of Mormon witnesses. He met three of them—David Whitmer, Martin Harris, and Hyrum Smith—when they passed his home in Illinois in August 1831. He walked several miles with them and "talked much" with them and other Saints for several days that summer. He wrote in his journal, "I took Hiram the brother of Joseph and we went into the woods and set down and talked together about 4 hours. I inquired into the particulars of the coming forth of the record, of the rise of the church and of its progress and upon the testimonies given to him." Of the next morning, William wrote, "I rose early and betook myself to earnest prayr to God to direct me into truth; and from all the light that I could gain by examinations searches and researches I was bound as an honest man to acknowledge the truth and Validity of the book of Mormon."[16]

William wrote in 1871 that the testimony of the witnesses "was no collusion. These men could not be mistaken. They either told the truth or they willfully lied. How shall we tell which?" he asked. "How shall we know?"[17] William then explained one of the ways he knew. It was one thing to be a Book of Mormon witness and a believer when the cost was relatively low. But two years after William first heard and believed the witnesses in 1831, the stakes were much higher. A mob offered a cash reward to anyone who would bring them William and Oliver Cowdery, who fled when they heard the news. Days later they met David Whitmer in the woods. William told what happened next:

> I said to them, "brethren I never have seen an open vision in my life, but you men say you have, and therefore you positively know. Now you know that our lives are in danger every hour, if the mob can only catch us. Tell me in the fear of God, is that book of Mormon true?" Cowdery looked at me with solemnity depicted in his face, and said, "Brother William, God sent his holy angel to declare the truth of the translation of it to us, and therefore we <u>know</u>. And though the mob kill us, yet we must die declaring its truth." David said, "Oliver has told you the solemn truth, for we could not be deceived. I most truly declare to you its truth!" Said I, boys I believe you, I can see no object for you to tell me falsehood now, when our lives are endangered. Eight men testify also to handling that sacred pile of plates, from which Joseph Smith read off the translation of that heavenly Book.[18]

William told about what happened to one of those eight witnesses, Hiram Page, at about the same time he and Oliver and David hid in the woods. A gang of young men ran Hiram down "and commenced beating and pounding him with whips and clubs. He begged, but there was no mercy. They said he was a damned Mormon, and they meant to beat him to death! But finally one of them said to him, if you will deny that damned book, we will let you go. Said he, how can I deny what I <u>know</u> to be true? Then they pounded him again."[19]

William served several missions, some as an Apostle, before becoming deeply disaffected later in the 1830s. Then he spent forty years frustrated by what he simultaneously loved and hated about the restored gospel before he received a letter from a Salt Lake City antagonist named James Cobb, who wrote to William assuming he would find an ally. William wrote back:

> "When I thoroughly examine a subject and settle my mind, then higher evidence must be introduced before I change. I have set to my seal that the Book of Mormon is a true, divine record and it will require more evidence than I have ever seen to ever shake me relative to its purity I have read many 'Exposes.' I have seen all their arguments. But my evidences are above them all!" He explained further, "When a man goes at the Book of M. he touches the apple of my eye. He fights against truth—against purity—against light—against the purist, or one of the truest, purist books on earth. I have more confidence in the Book of Mormon than any book of this wide earth![20]

William McLellin then described his own repeated readings of the Book of Mormon and noted his personal experiences with its witnesses. "When I first joined the church in 1831," he wrote, "soon I became acquainted with all the Smith family and the Whitmer family, and I heard all their testimonies, which agreed in the main points; and I believed them then and I believe them yet. But I don't believe the many stories (contradictory) got up since, for I individually know many of them are false."[21]

In his letter to James Cobb and elsewhere, William McLellin stated what he knew and how he knew it. His way of knowing was compelling, composed of his own careful, deep, enduring study, prayer, triangulating interviews of witnesses, and obeying the teachings of the Book of Mormon. Over time and by seeking out of the best books by study and also by faith, people come to know in the way Lucy Mack Smith, Rebecca Swain Williams, Sally Bradford Parker, and William McLellin knew. People who have that knowledge know how they know. They cannot explain away the Book of Mormon either intellectually or spiritually.

Those of us who do not yet know in that way can make the same soul-satisfying choices that Rebecca Williams, Sally Parker, and William McLellin did (though we will come back to William McLellin's story at a later point in this book). We can choose to believe in the direct statements of all the eyewitnesses of Book of Mormon translation and trust their demonstrably lifelong commitments to the book. True, this choice requires us to have faith in the marvelous, the ministering of actual angels, spiritual eyes and second sight, miraculous translation, and gold plates, but it does not require us to ignore or reject the historical record to reconcile the facts of the Book of Mormon with our own skepticism.

11.

Another Testament of Jesus Christ

On June 11, 1829, Joseph Smith filed for copyright of the Book of Mormon in a court in Utica, New York. With his application he filed a copy of the title page, which read, "The Book of Mormon: An Account Written by the Hand of Mormon upon Plates Taken from the Plates of Nephi."

In 1982, The Church of Jesus Christ of Latter-day Saints added the subtitle *Another Testament of Jesus Christ* to the Book of Mormon. Let's slow down and consider how consequential it is to claim—as the Book of Mormon title page does—that Jesus is the Christ. It is not simply saying that the God of Israel existed. Or that Jesus lived. It is saying that they are the same being, and that being is the promised Messiah, and that the believers who lived before He came knew to expect Him. The truth that the God of Israel is the Jewish Messiah—or Christ—and is the same as the Christian Savior—and that all of them are Jesus of Nazareth—is the restoration of lost knowledge. The Book of Mormon title page says the book exists to convince everyone that the God of Abraham was the babe of Bethlehem.

We may wonder if the Bible does not do that job. Or we may take for granted that people know—have always known—that hundreds of years before Christ, prophets knew and taught and testified that the Son of God would be born of a virgin and save the world from sin and death. But that is hardly common knowledge. Latter-day Saints know that because the Book of Mormon restores it. The Bible alone is not sufficient for the job of conflating Jesus of Nazareth with the Holy One of Israel.

Alexander Campbell (1788–1866) lived during the same period as Joseph Smith. He was a Reformed Baptist minister who knew the Bible well. He even translated the New Testament. Campbell concluded from his study of the scriptures that Christianity needed to be restored, and he believed that he was the one to do it. He began publishing the *Millennial Harbinger* newspaper in January 1830, a few months before the Book of Mormon was published and the Church of Jesus Christ was restored. The heading of *Millennial Harbinger* included Revelation 14:6–7: "And I saw another angel fly in the midst of heaven, having the everlasting gospel to preach unto them that dwell on the earth, and to every nation, and kindred, and tongue, and people, Saying with a loud voice, Fear God, and give glory to him; for the hour of his judgment is come: and worship him that made heaven, and earth, and the sea, and the fountains of waters."

Many of Campbell's followers, including Lydia Clisbee Partridge, Parley Pratt, Elizabeth Ann Smith Whitney, Sidney Rigdon, and others, became converted by the Book of Mormon in the fall of 1830. The February 1831 issue of Cambell's *Millennial Harbinger* included an article titled "Delusions," a detailed review of the Book of Mormon. *Delusions* was published as a pamphlet in 1832. It was the very first book (though hardly the last) aimed at undermining the Book of Mormon.

Campbell thought it was absurd that the Book of Mormon says that Jews like Nephi were Christians long before the birth of Jesus Christ. When the Book of Mormon was published in 1830, no one thought of people who lived before Christ as Christians.

Christians in the days of Alexander Campbell and Joseph Smith read prophecies of a coming Christ (Messiah) in the Old Testament, and Matthew's gospel and John's both emphasize that Jesus was the Christ. But people did not think of Adam and Eve, Abraham, Moses, and Isaiah as Christians, because long before the 1800s the Hebrew Bible (the Old Testament) did not include any passage that explicitly identified the God of Israel as Jesus of Nazareth. There is nothing in the Bible like the crystal-clear teachings given by Nephi, Benjamin, Abinadi, Alma, and Samuel before the Savior's earthly ministry. They taught that the God of Israel—the one who called Moses—is the baby born in Bethlehem, raised in Nazareth, and crucified in Jerusalem.

The Book of Mormon and Alexander Campbell talked past each other. Campbell said everyone knows that people who lived before Jesus knew nothing of Jesus, so the Book of Mormon cannot be accurate. The Book of Mormon says that because everyone (Campbell, for example) thinks they know that people who lived before Jesus knew nothing of Him, it has come forth to educate them otherwise. Jacob might have wondered how Campbell completely missed his point. "For this intent have we written these things," Jacob says, "that they may know that we knew of Christ, and we had a hope of his glory, many hundred years before his coming, and not only we ourselves had a hope of his glory, but also all the holy prophets which were before us. Behold, they worshiped the Father in his name" (Jacob 4:4–5).

When the Book of Mormon went on sale in March 1830, the first pages included the title page text twice. Joseph's manuscript history tells where that text came from:

> The Title Page of the Book of Mormon is a literal translation, taken from the very last leaf, on the left hand side of the collection or book of plates, which contained the record which has been translated; and not by any means the language of the whole running the same as all Hebrew writing in general; and that, said Title Page is not by any means a modern composition either of mine or of any other man's who has lived or does live in this generation. . . . [it] is a genuine and literal translation of the Title Page of the Original Book of Mormon, as recorded on the plates.[1]

Lehi and his posterity did not know in 600 BC that Jesus would be the Christ. They learned that as the Book of Mormon proceeds. Lehi learned about a Messiah or Christ figure who was followed by twelve (see 1 Nephi), suggesting Jesus and His apostles, but this link is implicit, not explicit.

Nephi learned more when he sought and received revelation about the meaning of his father's dream—including seeing a virgin from Nazareth with a child who was the Son of God (see 1 Nephi 11). But it is not until 2 Nephi 10 when we learn, as Nephi's brother Jacob learned, that the Redeemer they anticipated would be called Christ (see 2 Nephi 10). Nephi made sure to include that part in his record, and to add to it his own growing understanding, hoping to prove to his people "that save Christ should come all men must perish" (2 Nephi 11:6). That, Nephi tells us in 2 Nephi 11, is why he quoted and paraphrased so much of Isaiah.

Nephi knew from studying Isaiah and from his own revelations that salvation would only come through the grace of Christ, and that the law of Moses was given to point people to Christ (see 2 Nephi 25). Mormon made sure to record King Benjamin's address, which includes many specific teachings about the Savior (see Mosiah 3). A major reason Mormon included the whole story of Abinadi is to show how he knew—as Noah and his priests didn't— that the Messiah of whom Isaiah prophesied was Jesus Christ. The last words of Abinadi's discourse are, "If ye teach the law of Moses, also teach that it is a shadow of those things which are to come— Teach them that redemption cometh through Christ the Lord" (Mosiah 16:14–15). Later, Alma taught some of the most beautiful truths about the nature and extent of the Savior's Atonement and His redeeming and healing power (see Alma 7; 36). Finally, to Israelites who had been exiled from their promised land, and hoped for centuries on the promise of Christ, the Son of God descended out of heaven and said:

> Behold, I am Jesus Christ, whom the prophets testified shall come into the world.
>
> And behold, I am the light and the life of the world; and I have drunk out of that bitter cup which the Father hath given me, and have glorified the Father in taking upon me the sins of the world, in the which I have suffered the will of the Father in all things from the beginning. . . . Arise and come forth unto me, that ye may thrust your hands into my side, and

also that ye may feel the prints of the nails in my hands and in my feet, *that ye may know that I am the God of Israel,* and the God of the whole earth, and have been slain for the sins of the world. (3 Nephi 11:10–11, 14)

Then Moroni buried that knowledge in the ground, and it came forth nearly two millennia later to restore lost knowledge and a broken covenant.

President Russell M. Nelson invited us to imagine what our lives would be like without the Book of Mormon. Joseph Smith thought about that awful possibility for a few terrible months early in 1828. He had given the translation manuscript to Martin Harris, who had lost it. Joseph had disobeyed God, and he feared that he had ruined the transmission of the sacred record. In the revelation now known as Doctrine and Covenants 3, the Lord rebuked Joseph, invited him to repent, and taught him more about why the plates had been so painstakingly preserved:

For this very purpose are these plates preserved, which contain these records—that the promises of the Lord might be fulfilled, which he made to his people; And that the Lamanites might come to the knowledge of their fathers, and that they might know the promises of the Lord, and that they may believe the gospel and rely upon the merits of Jesus Christ, and be glorified through faith in his name, and that through their repentance they might be saved. (Doctrine and Covenants 3:19–20)

Alexander Campbell had only contempt for the Book of Mormon. He and others have assailed it for nearly two centuries. Mark Twain quipped that it was chloroform in print and did a superficial analysis of it. "If Joseph Smith composed this book, the act was a miracle," he wrote, then added, "Keeping awake while he did it was, at any rate."[2] That is funny, but neither Campbell nor Twain wrote anything as consequential as the Book of Mormon. We could concede Twain his point that the Book of Mormon can be tedious reading, but he missed the book's point. Maybe he did not read the title page. Though it is full of impressive, ancient literary forms, the Book of Mormon does not exist to win literary awards. The Book of Mormon was written, preserved, and translated by the power of God to convince everyone that God has restored His covenant and it is mediated by Jesus. He is everyone's Christ, always has been, and always will be. The Book of Mormon does that job intentionally and brilliantly. The Book of Mormon is another testament of Jesus Christ.

Ann Marsh Abbott learned that from her brother, Thomas, who was led by the Lord from Boston, Massachusetts, to Palmyra, New York, where he got a few pages of the Book of Mormon fresh from the press as it was being printed. Ann and her husband Lewis believed the Book of Mormon and embraced the covenant it declared. So they gathered with covenant Israel. They moved to Ohio with the Saints, then to the divinely designated center place of the gathering in Missouri: Zion. But Ann and her family were driven out by hateful men, first across the Missouri River, then out of Missouri altogether. In that process her brother Thomas, President of the Quorum of the Twelve Apostles, testified against Joseph Smith and left the covenant.[3]

Ann never did. Neither violent mob attacks on her family or widespread discontent and opposition inside the Savior's Church derailed her covenant faithfulness. She wrote to her siblings, "Through all our trials and afflictions our faith is not lessened but strengthened." The Book of Mormon was her anchor. She expressed her love for Thomas and the rest of her family and her desires for their happiness. She invited her loved ones to think slowly and seek learning by study and by faith out of the very best book. "The Plan of Salvation you can know for yourself," she testified, "if you will read the Book of Mormon without prejudice." After many years away, Thomas remembered that he knew that too, and he returned to the covenant and The Church of Jesus Christ.[4]

PROBLEMS
SOLVED

12.

How the Restoration Resolves Priesthood Problems

The ongoing Restoration resolves problems. This chapter is about how the Restoration resolves priesthood problems. Jesus Christ called, ordained, and authorized apostles. He gave them access to His priesthood—power to act in His name to do His work. He also gave them keys—the commission to use the priesthood to accomplish His purposes. Those apostles called a few other apostles and ordained them, but they prophesied that the Savior's church would go into the wilderness, and then they watched as it did. Along the way, they were killed or exiled. So by about AD 100, the only apostle who remained on earth was John, and he was exiled to an island in the Aegean Sea. That gives us the first priesthood problem:

1. There were no apostles to exercise the priesthood and its keys.

Some Christian seekers, including Roger Williams (1603–1683), recognized this problem. A neighbor of Roger's—a fellow seventeenth-century Baptist—wrote that "He brake off from his Society, and declared at large the Ground and Reasons of it: That their Baptism could not be right, because It was not Administred by an Apostle. After that he set upon a Way of Seeking . . ."[1]

A biographer of Roger Williams wrote that he compared "Christianity in its authentic form" with the church of his own day, "a church scattered in the wilderness," and concluded that in the "latter days" the glorious church would be restored. So "Williams now awaited the apostles whose preaching would bring that plan to realization."[2]

How did Joseph Smith become aware of this priesthood problem? How did he become the apostle that Roger Williams and others waited for? Imagine that you are seventeen-year-old Joseph Smith. You pray for forgiveness. You are answered by an angel sent from God with a staggering learning curve for you. It includes this prophesy:

> For behold, the day cometh that shall burn as an oven, and all the proud, yea, and all that do wickedly shall burn as stubble; for they that come shall burn them, saith the Lord of Hosts, that it shall leave them neither root nor branch. (Joseph Smith—History 1:37)

And it includes this promise:

> I will reveal unto you the Priesthood, by the hand of Elijah the prophet, before the coming of the great and dreadful day of the Lord. . . . And he shall plant in the hearts of the children the promises made to the fathers, and the hearts of the children shall turn to their fathers. If it were not so, the whole earth would be utterly wasted at his coming. (Joseph Smith—History 1:38-39)

That September night in 1823 when Moroni first appeared to Joseph might have been the first time Joseph ever heard the word *priesthood*. What is it? What does it have to do with roots and branches? Why the urgency in Moroni's message? President Russell M. Nelson explained the urgency in a way that is clear in our present day, but only because it became clear to Joseph over time—line by line and precept by precept (see Isaiah 28:13; Doctrine and Covenants 128:21). President Nelson taught:

> The Atonement enabled the purpose of the Creation to be accomplished. Eternal life, made possible by the Atonement, is the supreme purpose of the Creation. To phrase that statement in its negative form, if families were not sealed in holy temples, the whole earth would be utterly wasted.[3]

That gives us the second priesthood problem:

2. Unless families get sealed by the priesthood, the creation will be for nothing at the Lord's coming. In 1820, there was no one around who had power (priesthood) to seal families or the commission (keys) to do so.

With Moroni as a mentor, Joseph worked hard for several years to obtain the plates, then for a few more years to get the writing inscribed on them translated and published. While translating the Book of Mormon in May 1829, Joseph Smith and Oliver Cowdery discovered the third priesthood problem:

3. The Savior declared that unless a person makes and keeps the baptismal covenant (mediated by someone with priesthood), they are damned. Joseph and Oliver did not know anyone with priesthood who could baptize them.

The Lord resolved this priesthood problem the same day: May 15, 1829. As Joseph and Oliver were praying in the Pennsylvania woods, the now-resurrected man who baptized Jesus appeared, gave Joseph and Oliver priesthood, and commissioned them to use it to make the baptismal covenant. It is easy for people who have heard that story many times to be ho-hum about it. Even Joseph's description of it is matter-of-fact:

> The messenger who visited us on this occasion and conferred this Priesthood upon us, said that his name was John, the same that is called John the Baptist in the New Testament, and that he acted under the direction of Peter, James and John, who held the keys of the Priesthood of Melchizedek, which Priesthood, he said, would in due time be conferred on us, and that I should be called the first Elder of the Church, and he (Oliver Cowdery) the second. It was on the fifteenth day of May, 1829, that we were ordained under the hand of this messenger, and baptized. (Joseph Smith—History 1:72)

Be careful not to lose a sense of awe just because of how straightforwardly Joseph testified that he was ordained by the man who baptized Jesus and was executed some 1,800 years earlier. That solution is indicative of how spectacularly the Restoration resolves priesthood problems.

John the Baptist revealed the next priesthood problem:

4. Joseph and Oliver needed more priesthood to lay on hands for the gift of the Holy Ghost.

Joseph Smith and Oliver Cowdery testified that they received the Melchizedek Priesthood and were ordained apostles by Peter, James, and John. This solved the first and the fourth problem, but our records of it (or lack thereof) pose a different kind of problem—a problem of what we know and how. We have no record from Joseph or Oliver that narrates the experience of their ordination to the Melchizedek priesthood and the apostleship. They both recorded the fact that they received more priesthood from Peter, James, and John, who ordained them apostles, but the records we have do not specify when or where.[4] That limits what we know about priesthood restoration.

The accounts we have from Joseph and Oliver include a revelation to Joseph, first published in 1835, in which the Lord describes "Peter, and James, and John, whom I have sent unto you, by whom I have ordained you and confirmed you to be apostles" (Doctrine and Covenants 27:12); a Joseph Smith sermon from about 1839 in which he declared that "the Savior, Moses, & Elias—gave the Keys to Peter, James & John . . . [and] they gave it up" to him;[5] and an 1842 musing about the time when Joseph and Oliver met "Peter, James, and John in the wilderness"[6] near the Susquehannah River and they declared "themselves as possessing the keys of the kingdom" (Doctrine and Covenants 128:20). They and other angels transmitted to Joseph Smith and Oliver Cowdery "the power of their priesthood" (Doctrine and Covenants 128:21). Joseph and Oliver in turn ordained the Twelve Apostles in 1835. Oliver told them, "You have been ordained to the Holy Priesthood. You have received it from those who had their power and authority from an angel."[7]

Joseph and Oliver also recorded interpretive memories that make it hard for us to disentangle what they knew at the time of an event (like their ordination by John the Baptist on May 15, 1829) from what they grew to know and understand later. This makes it hard to grasp all these years later that Joseph did not know all that is now known about priesthood. He did not know or understand all that is now known when Moroni began teaching him, or even after he was ordained to the priesthoods, or even after he received a hundred revelations, or organized the Savior's church, or even after angels including Elijah brought him the priesthood Moroni mentioned. It is therefore easy to think too fast and make assumptions looking backward about how things have always been that Joseph did not make looking forward.

Joseph Smith's Manuscript History contributes to the problem of not knowing as much as we would like to about priesthood restoration because it does not include an account of Peter, James, and John restoring priesthood, but it also describes the fifth priesthood problem:[8]

5. Joseph and Oliver did not know how to exercise the priesthood to organize and lead the Savior's church.

Joseph's Manuscript History says they "made this matter a subject of humble prayer." After one "solemn and fervent prayer" in the Whitmers' home, the Lord revealed that Joseph should ordain Oliver Cowdery an elder in The Church of Jesus Christ, and that Oliver should ordain Joseph to the same office, but they should wait until they gathered the baptized believers, received their consent and sustaining vote, and took the sacrament together. Then, after their ordinations as elders of the Savior's church, they should confirm the baptized believers as members and "attend to the laying on of hands for the gift of the Holy Ghost." Joseph and Oliver obeyed the revelation on April 6, 1830, when they were sustained and then ordained as the elders of the Savior's church.[9]

The next major priesthood problem became known to Joseph in

the Lord's September 1832 revelation (what later became Doctrine and Covenants 84), which began with a prophecy that a temple would be built in that generation. Then there is a long digression in the revelation that may be the most important part of it. In it, the Lord revealed a history of priesthood as part of an explanation about why priesthood is vital. The revelation forges a link between temple ordinances and priesthood power. It gives us the sixth priesthood problem:

> 6. Everyone needs an endowment of priesthood power in order to regain God's presence and stay there. That power is only available in the ordinances of the Melchizedek priesthood.

That was news to Joseph, who had received revelations about endowments for Moses and others and a promise that the Lord would endow the Saints with power, but probably did not yet know how to give the ordinances that endow their recipients with power to regain God's presence and abide there.

Here is a review of how the Restoration resolves priesthood problems:

Problem 1: There were no apostles.

Solution: Apostolic angels Peter, James, and John ordained Joseph and Oliver as apostles and commissioned them to ordain other apostles.

Problem 2: Unless families get sealed by the priesthood, the creation will have been for nothing at the Lord's coming, and there was no one empowered and authorized by God to seal families.

Solution: A later chapter in this book will tell this story, so keep reading.

Problem 3: Unless a person makes and keeps the baptismal covenant, mediated by someone commissioned to do so with the priesthood, they are damned. They have not made the covenant that binds them to Jesus Christ and makes His salvation theirs.

Solution: John the Baptist ordained Joseph and Oliver as Aaronic priests and commissioned them to baptize.

Problem 4: Joseph and Oliver needed more priesthood to lay on hands for the gift of the Holy Ghost.

Solution: This problem was solved along with Problem 1 when Peter, James, and John ordained Joseph and Oliver as apostles.

Problem 5: Joseph and Oliver did not know how to exercise the priesthood to organize the Savior's church.

Solution: They sought and received the Lord's directions by revelation, then followed them carefully.

Problem 6: Everyone needs an endowment of God's power to regain God's presence and stay there. A later chapter of this book tells how the Restoration resolved this problem, so keep reading.

Will Joseph get Priesthood Problems 2 and 6 resolved before his enemies kill him? The stakes are so high: If families aren't sealed before the Savior's coming, the earth is wasted. And if we are not endowed with priesthood power, we cannot get back to God's presence and stay there. The opposition is immense. Bad guys are closing in. Soon Joseph will be in the clutches of enemies conspiring to execute him. It is then that he comes face-to-face with what may be the most challenging priesthood problem of all:

Problem 7: It is the nature and disposition of almost all men to exercise power unrighteously. And priesthood is power that cannot be controlled or even handled unrighteously (see Doctrine and Covenants 121).

The maxim that absolute power corrupts absolutely is wrong. The corrupting cancer does not grow from having "all power" (Doctrine and Covenants 132:20). It grows from a little power exercised unrighteously—by covering one's sins, gratifying one's pride or vain ambitions, or controlling or compelling anyone else in any degree of unrighteousness. Sadly, that is what most people do, so they never obtain absolute power. The people who become exalted with all power (glory, intelligence, life, light, law, truth) only accumulate it by degrees when they make choices to trade their unrighteous nature and disposition for real love, kindness, pure knowledge, no hypocrisy, no guile, virtue, holiness, and charity for everyone in and out of the Church. People who do that accumulate power or priesthood until they can confidently be in God's presence (see Doctrine and Covenants 121:34–46).

Priesthood is bigger and better than we may have imagined. It is God's power, and God is resolving serious problems by restoring priesthood. He has done that. He is doing that. He will continue to do that. But whether we obtain power in the priesthood depends on our choices to covenant with God by His power to be endowed with His power, sealed by His power, and changed by His power.

13.

William McLellin's Love/Hate Relationship with Revelation

If we think fast about the Lord's revelations to Joseph Smith, we might assume that *if* God spoke to him, it would have been in flawless English (whatever that is), and that we have God's original words precisely as they were originally given. Joseph Smith did not assume that, and the Lord said in revelation that it does not work that way.

Here are some verifiable facts: We do not have most of Joseph's original revelation texts. We have a few originals, many other copies, and two manuscript revelation books into which revelations were copied. These manuscripts and the books that were printed from them evidence editing throughout the process. How should we interpret those facts?

Hopefully we will choose to interpret them with an eye of faith. This chapter tells the story of what William McLellin knew about the Lord's revelations to Joseph, how he knew it, and how he chose to interpret the facts to cope with his cognitive dissonance—the awful tension he felt when the gap between what he believed and how he behaved was too wide.

Let's start by deciding what we mean by *revelation*. Elder David A. Bednar gave this definition: "Revelation is communication from God to His children on the earth."[1] Religion scholar David Carpenter added that revelation is "a process mediated through language."[2] Both of those definitions accurately describe the Lord's revelations to Joseph Smith. To understand their implications, we need a basic understanding of communication theory:

- An encoder sends a signal.
- A decoder receives the signal.
- Noise between them hinders perfect transmission and reception.

Communication noise is not necessarily audible. Sound can interrupt revelation, but other kinds of noise hinder communication too:

- Semantic noise happens when the encoder sends signals that the decoder lacks the power to decipher. Imagine Joseph receiving revelation in Spanish or computer programming code.
- Psychological noise happens when a decoder's mental state prevents accurate interpretation of the signal.
- Assumptions, prejudices, preconceived notions, or emotions can cause communication noise that prevents an accurate interpretation of an encoded signal—a revelation. In other words, when it comes to revelation, thinking fast is noisy.

Beginning with Elder Bednar's teaching that revelation is communication from God to us, how might communication noise impact revelation? Considering Professor Carpenter's point that revelation is a process mediated through language, how might language be a noisy mediator? How might being open to revelation as a *process* help us hear Him despite the noise?

Revelation comes from a flawless, divine encoder, but mortals are the decoders. All kinds of communication noise prevents us from receiving revelation perfectly. The Lord could send flawless signals, but neither Joseph Smith or any other mortal—prophet or otherwise—has been a perfect decoder. All of this means that a person can receive revelation and not understand it. When that happens, it is not because God encoded the revelation wrong or badly. It is because noise of some kind or another disrupted the decoding.

What could happen if God revealed the answers to five of your secret questions about your personal life and what He wants you to do? Could there be anything negative about that? Let's find out.

When William McLellin was in his twenties, he was a schoolteacher in Paris, Illinois, not far from the Mississippi River, where death has just robbed him of his wife, Cynthia Ann, and their newborn daughter.

One morning he heard that two men were traveling through on their way to Zion in Missouri. They had a book called the Book of Mormon. They claimed it was revelation from God. They planned to preach in a sugar tree grove south of town.

William saddled his horse and got there as fast as he could, "anxious to see and hear" the missionaries.[3] He learned their names were Harvey Whitlock and David Whitmer. Harvey told why he believed the Book of Mormon to be divine revelation, and William thought he expounded "the Gospel the plainest" he ever heard in his life.

David then stood and testified to "having seen an Holy Angel who had made known the truth of this record to him." William pondered the strange things he heard. He invited the missionaries to preach again the next day, then he started following them from town to town, asking them questions between their preaching appointments. They told him Joseph Smith was a prophet, that he was on his way to Jackson County, Missouri, just like them, though by a different route. He begged them to stay one week and, in that time, he finished his teaching obligation, settled his affairs, and joined "the strange preachers." He even took them to Cynthia Ann's grave, "and there they seemed to mourn with me for the loss of my dearest friend and her blessed little infant."

For two and a half weeks, William rode hard until he arrived in Independence. He stopped for breakfast, fed his horse, and asked the villagers "about those people they call Mormonites." They were generally honest, came the reply, "but very much deluded by Smith and others." Still, William felt "anxious to see them and examine for myself."

He met Martin Harris, Bishop Edward Partridge, and his counselors, but, to his disappointment, Joseph Smith had come and gone. William prayed with the Saints and saw love, peace, harmony, and humility in them. He felt his weakness keenly. He and Hyrum Smith then went for a walk in the woods, sat down, and talked for hours. William asked Hyrum all about the Book of Mormon and how it came forth, the rise of the Church, and his experiences. In the evening, William worshipped with the Saints.

The next morning, Sunday, August 20, 1831, he rose early and prayed earnestly, asking God to direct him, and he realized that he was "bound as an honest man to acknowledge the truth and Validity of the book of Mormon, and also that I had found the people of the

Lord—The Living Church of Christ." He asked Hyrum to baptize him. He felt happy and calm that day, but in the evening began to feel sick inside. He did not doubt "the truth of the things which I had embraced." Rather, he feared for his salvation because he had sins and weaknesses no one else knew about, and not even baptism and the undeniable feeling of the Holy Spirit made him feel as clean as he hoped it would. Still, he saw more holiness and beauty and felt more peace and happiness than he ever had before. His motives were purer, and he was better than before. He wanted to be ordained and preach the good news to everyone.

Hyrum Smith and Bishop Partridge ordained William later that day, and he felt "very solemn while taking this charge upon me. Yet I was willing to proclaim in my weakness, the glorious gospel of the great Redeemer." He walked all the way to Ohio with his brethren, preaching all along the way, and there, at a conference on October 25, he "first saw brother Joseph the Seer," and he was ordained a high priest. After the conference, William McLellin walked with Joseph to a neighboring town, planning to prove to himself forevermore that Joseph was indeed a prophet. So when he arrived at the Johnson home, where Joseph and Emma and their adopted twins were living, he asked Joseph to seek a revelation from the Lord for him.[4]

Joseph dictated the Lord's answer as William scribed it. The revelation is now Doctrine and Covenants 66. At the end of William's manuscript, he wrote "Joseph Smith, Revelator," and underlined it heavily. When he wrote this, William McLellin knew—knew as few other people have ever known—that Joseph Smith was a revelator. In William's journal entry for October 29, 1831, he wrote, "This day the Lord condecended to hear my prayr and give me a revelation of his will, through his prophet or seer (Joseph)—And these are the words I wrote from his mouth." William then copied the revelation into his journal.[5]

Seventeen years later, William testified that this revelation included the Lord's intimate answers to five secret questions that no one else knew. Just a week after writing Doctrine and Covenants 66, William was part of a very important meeting with Joseph and other leaders, deciding what to do with his revelations. They were discussing the Book of Commandments and Revelations. At the time it was the only archive of Joseph's revelation texts. Original manuscripts of revelations like William's manuscript of section 66 were circulating, but they had been transcribed into the Book of Commandments and Revelations by John Whitmer (see Doctrine and Covenants 47).

The council discussed the pros and cons of publishing the revelations in this book. Try to appreciate their dilemma. They had more than sixty revelation texts, and they were mainly in the first-person voice of Jesus Christ. They revealed the doctrines of and tactics for the Savior's great commission to take his gospel to all people, the gathering of Israel, the building of Zion, and the endowment of power needed to regain God's presence. The Saints needed to know what was in these revelations. But the revelations also said the Saints' neighbors were idolatrous, their culture was deeply flawed, calamities awaited everyone who would not repent, and that Missourians were *enemies*. To complicate matters more, the revelations were written in what Joseph would later call a crooked, broken, scattered, and imperfect language.[6] Professor Carpenter called revelation a process mediated through language. Joseph called his language a "narrow prison."[7]

Everyone in the council in November 1831 must have recognized that they were being asked to support a poorly educated farmer in his mid-twenties who was planning to publish ten thousand copies of revelations that were not properly punctuated, whose spelling was not standardized, and whose grammar was inconsistent. The men were discussing whether to publish yet another book of scripture— and this one didn't even have the advantage of being ancient—in a Protestant-dominated country where the Bible was widely believed to be all the scripture there would ever be.

Joseph's history tells us that the council engaged in a discussion "concerning revelations and language."[8] Undaunted, Joseph told the council that "the Lord has bestowed a great blessing upon us in giving commandments and revelations." He asked for their support in getting them published. He testified that the contents of such a book should "be prized by this Conference to be worth to the Church the riches of the whole Earth."[9] Joseph was sure that his revelation texts were both divine and imperfect. The brethren in the council could see that the revelation texts were imperfect. Joseph promised them they could know they were divine as well.

Just a few days earlier, Joseph had prophesied that if the Saints could "all come together with one heart and one mind in perfect faith the vail might as well be rent to day as next week or any other time."[10] Seeking confirmation of the revelations, the brethren tried to rend the veil like the brother of Jared in the Book of Mormon. They failed. Joseph asked the Lord why, and he received the answer in Doctrine and Covenants section 67. In that revelation, the Lord assured the Church leaders that He had heard their prayers and knew all the desires in their hearts. "There were fears in your hearts," He told them, and "this is the reason that ye did not receive" (Doctrine and Covenants 67:3). He then testified of the truthfulness of the Book of Commandments and Revelations. The brethren had been watching Joseph, listening to him, observing his imperfections, and wishing secretly, or perhaps even assuming, that they could do a better job than he. The Lord offered them the opportunity.

He told them to have the wisest man in the council (or any of them who cared to) mimic the simplest revelation in this book. The Lord told the elders that if they succeeded in composing a pseudo-revelation text equal to the least of Joseph's, then they could justifiably say that they did not know the revelations were true. But if they failed, the Lord said He would hold them guilty unless they testified to the veracity of the revelations. The Lord's words in section 67 led the men to recognize that whatever imperfections the revelation texts showed—communicated as they were in "their language" (Doctrine and Covenants 1:24), not God's—they conformed to divine laws, were full of holy principles, and were just, virtuous, and good. They could conclude on those criteria that, though clothed in a "crooked broken scattered and imperfect language," such revelations came from God.[11]

Joseph's history and other sources tell us how the council acted on the instructions in section 67 and became willing to testify before the world that the revelations were true—but not flawless—texts. William McLellin "endeavored to write a commandment like unto one of the least of the Lord's, but failed."[12] Joseph had asked the council "what testimony they were willing to attach to these commandments which should shortly be sent to the world."[13] Several of the men stood and expressed willingness to tell the world they knew that the revelations came from the Lord. Joseph revealed a statement for them to sign as witnesses. It says in part, "We the undersigners feel willing to bear testimony to all the world of mankind to every creature upon all the face of all the Earth <&> upon the Islands of the Sea that god hath born record to our souls through the Holy Ghost shed forth upon us that these commandments are given by inspiration of God & are profitable for all men & are verily true we give this testimony unto the world the Lord being my <our> helper."[14]

William McLellin and four other men signed the testimony. A committee of the Church's best writers drafted a preface for the Book of Revelations, but it was inadequate. The Lord ended up revealing His own preface through Joseph. Sidney Rigdon sat down by the window, dipped his quill in an inkwell, and wrote as Joseph spoke the words slowly, pausing regularly for Sidney's sake. Then Sidney read the words back to Joseph, who would correct them or pronounce them correct, and then continue. But they are not Joseph's words. They are the Savior's words. He called them "*my* preface unto the book of *my* commandments" (Doctrine and Covenants 1:6; emphasis added).

Yet they are Joseph's words after all, because in them the Savior explains why He gave the revelations to Joseph in crooked, broken, scattered, imperfect language: "Behold, I am God and have spoken it; these commandments are of me, and were given unto my servants in their weakness, after the manner of their language, that they might come to understanding" (Doctrine and Covenants 1:24).

That important verse is the Lord's rationale for the flawed, noisy form of His revelations to the Saints. He could reveal in a pure language; the Saints just would not be able to hear Him if He did. So He reveals in ways that accommodate our weakness, using our noisy language, knowing that if we work hard at revelation, we will come to understand it over time. President Russell M. Nelson pleaded with us "to increase your spiritual capacity to receive revelation."

He admonished, "Choose to do the spiritual work required to enjoy the gift of the Holy Ghost and hear the voice of the Spirit more frequently and more clearly."[15]

With a clear sense that the revelation texts were both human and divine, the council resolved that Joseph "correct those errors or mistakes which he may discover by the holy Spirit."[16] Joseph and others (including Oliver Cowdery, Sidney Rigdon, and the printer William Phelps) edited his revelation texts repeatedly, making changes for clarity—to minimize noise. Joseph welcomed the edits of those literate men; he just admonished them to "be careful not to alter the sense" of the revelation manuscripts.[17] Oliver Cowdery reported to the Saints on the progress of this process, saying that the revelation texts "are now correct," adding, "if not in every word, at least in principle."[18] Revising, amending, and expanding earlier revelation texts is the prerogative of prophets, and Joseph Smith considered ongoing revelation one of his major responsibilities—a way for him to "come to understanding" and to help the Saints do so (Doctrine and Covenants 1:24).

Some people have criticized the edits. One such effort is cleverly titled *Doctored Covenants*. Why all the changes? it asks. I and a few other people have spent decades sincerely seeking answers to that question, and we have found a lot of answers, though few people are interested in them.[19] The point of *Doctored Covenants* is not to understand the process of revelation but to insinuate that there is something wrong with the revelations, and therefore with The Church of Jesus Christ of Latter-day Saints.

Fascinatingly but not uniquely, William McLellin transitioned from being a believer in Joseph's revelations to being a critic of them. This is what we know about how that happened. Remember that a week before he tried unsuccessfully to compose a pseudo-revelation text, William McLellin wrote the original manuscript of section 66 as Joseph rendered the Lord's communication in the best words he could. William later testified that in this revelation the Lord answered every one of his intimate questions, which were unknown to Joseph. William subsequently reported to his relatives that he had spent about three weeks with Joseph, "and from my acquaintance then and until now I can truely say I believe him to be a man of God. A Prophet, a Seer and Revelater to the church of christ." Later in the same letter, William related, "We believe that Joseph Smith is a true Prophet or Seer of the Lord and that he <u>has</u> power and <u>does</u> receive revelations from God, and that these revelations when received are of divine Authority in the church of Christ."[20] William McLellin knew as well as anyone that Joseph received revelations, that they were both divine and human products, and that Joseph had been appointed by the Church to prepare them for publication, including by making inspired revisions.

William kept such detailed records that we know he struggled to do the things the Lord told him to do in answer to his five intimate questions. Joseph was returning from Missouri to Ohio when he heard that William had specifically disobeyed several of the Lord's commands in Doctrine and Covenants 66. Joseph vented in his June 6, 1832, letter to Emma that William's "conduct merits the disapprobation of every true follower of Christ. . . . I am not pleased to hear that William Mclelin has. . . . disobayed the voice of him who is altogether Lovely."[21] William was excommunicated, then quickly received back into fellowship before leaving on a mission with Parley Pratt early in 1833. Two years later, William was chosen as one of the twelve apostles. He left the church in 1836. His quorum members wrote to him, inviting him to "come home, come home." In 1837, he answered. "Can you, Will you forgive me?" he wrote. "Will Brother Joseph forgive me? And will the Church forgive me?"[22] The answer to all three questions was yes, but in 1838 Bishop Partridge convened a disciplinary council at which William answered charges of adultery:

> Said he had no confidence in the heads of the Church, beleiving they had transgressed, and got out of the way, and consequently <he> left of[f] praying and keeping the commandments of God, and went his own way, and indulged himself in his lustfull desires. But when he heard, that the first presidency, had made a general settlement and acknowleged their sins, he then began to pray again, and to keep the commandments of God. Though when interogated by Pres^t smith he said he had seen nothing out of the way himself but it was heresay, and thus he judged from heresay. But we are constrained to say, O!! foolish Man! what excuse is that thou renderest, for thy sins, that because thou hast heard of some mans transgression, that thou shouldest leave thy God, and forsake thy prayers, and turn to those things that thou knowest to be contrary to the will of God.[23]

By the autumn of 1838, William was eagerly allied with the Missourians who plundered the Saints and drove them from the state. He hated Joseph by then—hated that the Lord had ever answered his secret questions so specifically through his flawed prophet.

Joseph considered it "an awful responsibility to write in the name of the Lord," largely because he felt confined by the "total darkness of paper pen and Ink and a crooked broken scattered and imperfect

Language."[24] Joseph rightfully regarded his language as a deeply flawed medium for communication. Even so, the Lord consciously revealed the sections of the Doctrine and Covenants in language Joseph could come to understand so that we too could come, by a process, to understand (see Doctrine and Covenants 1:24). The Divine Encoder chose to communicate with His servants in their weakness in order to maximize their ability to comprehend. Joseph's revelation texts are not limited by the Lord who gave them but in the imperfect language available to His weak servants, who had to decode the divine messages with various kinds of noise inhibiting them.

In 1871, William McLellin asserted that Joseph Smith had lost power to act for God in 1834, after Joseph and others edited the revelation texts for publication. "Now if the Lord gave those revelations," William McLellin reasoned, "he said what he meant, and meant what he said."[25] Though he testified repeatedly with good evidence that Joseph's revelations were true, William assumed that he could decode a revelation immediately. But Joseph did not assume that. The Lord did not say it. Rather, the Lord said in Doctrine and Covenants 1:24: "Behold, I am God and have spoken it; these commandments are of me, and were given unto my servants in their weakness, after the manner of their language, that they might come to understanding."

Brigham Young thought slowly about this. He did not believe "that there is a single revelation, among the many God has given to the Church, that is perfect in its fullness. The revelations of God contain correct doctrine and principle, so far as they go; but it is impossible for the poor, weak, low, grovelling, sinful inhabitants of the earth to receive a revelation from the Almighty in all its perfections. He has to speak to us in a manner to meet the extent of our capacities."[26] William McLellin, on the other hand, assumed that Joseph could receive revelation flawlessly and communicate it perfectly, and that everyone would understand the full import and meaning of his revelations in an instant, like turning on a light switch rather than watching a sunrise.[27]

Those who, like William McLellin, argue for perfect scriptures (which is not a scriptural teaching) assume that divine communication is complete and perfect, that mortals can decode the divine without corruption. But revelation is communication that is mediated by the power of the Holy Ghost; the Holy Ghost is the perfect mediator of otherwise imperfect communication. Reading revelation texts by the power of the Holy Ghost (however flawed the language in which they are encoded, and however noisy the circumstances) and thinking about them carefully over time and in light of experience will enable us to "come to understanding" (Doctrine and Covenants 1:24).

Thinking slowly about revelation leads us to recognize it as a process by which we come to understand God. We think less about whether the Lord said what He meant and meant what He said and think more about whether we have understood what He meant and acted obediently on what He said. The question is not whether words were accurately written "with ink" or "on tablets of stone," but whether they were written "with the Spirit of the living God . . . on tablets of human hearts" (2 Corinthians 3:3, New Revised Standard Version).

14.

Reading the Bible Like Joseph Smith Did

Protestant professors often say that any text without context is pretext for a proof text. It means that when readers are ignorant of a scripture's origin, intent, and audience, that scripture can easily be misused to support claims that are not true. As a teenager who was anxious about his sins and salvation, Joseph Smith read the Bible in the context of proof texting:

> How to act I did not know and unless I could get more wisdom than I then had would never know, for the teachers of religion of the different sects understood the same passage of Scripture so differently as <to> destroy all confidence in settling the question by an appeal to the Bible.[1]

But that way of reading the Bible began to change one day as Joseph read in the Book of James. For the first time, he escaped the confines of Protestant culture, including the assumption that the Bible was the archive of all God ever said. Joseph felt the power of God's living word. "Never did any passage of scripture come with more power to the heart of man that this did at this time to mine," he remembered. "It seemed to enter with great force into every feeling of my heart" (Joseph Smith—History 1:12). He obeyed the revelation to ask God for more revelation, and that led to more revelation, more of God's word, more scripture. The restored scriptures that came through Joseph Smith provide the best context for reading the Bible. In other words, we can understand the Bible best if we think slowly about it, ask questions, and seek answers from other scriptures, including the Book of Mormon, the Doctrine and Covenants, and the Pearl of Great Price.

Many of Joseph's revelations came because his careful reading of the Bible raised questions to which he sought God's answers. Joseph began a close reading/revision of the Bible shortly after the Lord restored His church in 1830 (see Doctrine and Covenants 35). The Book of Moses came first. It blew open the doors to understanding who God is and why He does what He does, how He relates to his children, and how to understand Genesis and other parts of the Bible.

After revising Genesis in light of the Book of Moses, Joseph received the revelation in Doctrine and Covenants 45 in March 1831. It turned his attention to the New Testament. Joseph finished his revision of the whole Bible in 1833, but he never thought it was an urtext, meaning the original or earliest version. Joseph had a much broader sense of the concept of *restoration* than just taking the Bible or the Church back to its original state. There never was a perfect Bible, and Joseph didn't think he was creating one. Joseph did not think of the scriptures or any other part of the Restoration as if they were finished, complete, or no longer in need of revision or restoration. His Bible project was not a quest to produce the *product* of a perfect Bible. It was a *process* of learning from the Bible, and from the best available academic resources, and from the Lord's revelations.

Much like restoring a house, Joseph restored the Bible and the Savior's Church by keeping all the best elements of the original, getting rid of what did not work, and adding features that were not original (see Doctrine and Covenants 124:41).

In 1838, the prophet Joseph Smith confidently answered questions he was frequently asked about the Bible:

> *Question:* Is there anything in the Bible which licenses you to believe in revelation now a days.
>
> *Answer:* Is there anything that does not authorize us to believe so; if there is, we have, as yet, not been able to find it.
>
> *Question:* Is not the cannon of the Scriptures full.
>
> *Answer:* If it is, there is a great defect in the book, or else it would have said so.[2]

These confident answers show how the Lord's revelations to Joseph, beginning with the epiphany while reading James 1:5, helped him transcend the Protestant assumption about the Bible known as *sola scriptura*. This doctrine of the Protestant Reformation replaced the authority of the Catholic Pope with scripture, meaning the Bible. Protestant Christians declare that the Bible alone, not the Pope, is the highest authority and the ultimate arbiter of truth.

The problem with sola scriptura is the way it limits the God whose word the Bible is. The Methodist minister had sola scriptura in mind when he expressed contempt for Joseph's vision, saying it was of the devil and that real revelations were a thing of the past. But Joseph discovered that the Bible is brimming with invitations to seek and receive more revelation. Anyone who lacks wisdom can ask God and be answered, not upbraided. The Restoration teaches us that it's not God's most ancient word that is most authoritative. It is God's most recent word that prevails.

The Westminster Confession is a Protestant creed written in the 1640s. It declares the *sola scriptura* dogma in these words:

> The whole counsel of God, concerning all things necessary for His own glory, man's salvation, faith, and life, is either expressly set down in Scripture, or by good and necessary consequence may be deduced from Scripture: unto which nothing at any time is to be added, whether by new revelations of the Spirit, or traditions of men.[3]

The idea that God could not and would not amend the Bible with new revelations remains a dominant teaching of Protestantism today. The Restoration challenges sola scriptura and offers a better definition of scripture. *Scripture* and *Bible* are synonymous in unrestored Christianity. In restored Christianity, the Bible is scripture, but not all of it. In a November 1831 revelation to Joseph, the Lord taught that whatever is said by someone "when moved upon by the Holy Ghost shall be scripture" (Doctrine and Covenants 68:4). This revelation defines scripture as the Lord's will, mind, word, voice, and power. It does not confine scripture to the covers of any one book. And it disqualifies parts of the Bible as scripture.[4]

Joseph's notes say, "Malachi Correct, Finished on the 2d day of July 1833," but we would misunderstand Joseph if we interpreted that to mean that his reading and revising of the scriptures was finished, done, complete, no longer in need of revision, or no longer a springboard for revelation.[5] Rather, the Lord's revelations to Joseph confirmed both that the Bible is the word of God and that it is not sufficient or complete. The Bible is not *all* the word of God—meaning that not everything in it is God's word and that God's words are not all in it. The Lord's revelations to Joseph expand greatly on what is known from the Bible alone. But in revealing so much, the Lord did not indicate to Joseph that the revelations or scriptures were perfect or static, even when they were "finished." The Book of Mormon title page, for example, says that the book includes both "the mistakes of men" and "the things of God." God is okay with that, and we can choose to be okay with it too.

The Restoration teaches us to seek more revelation, more scripture. James 1:5 opened the Restoration, and Joseph Smith learned to read the Bible as an open invitation to seek and receive revelation.

15.

Scrolls, Mummies, and the Book of Abraham

There is a raging controversy over the Book of Abraham. One faction interprets the facts to mean that Joseph made up the Book of Abraham. Another interprets the facts to mean he translated it from writing that was on papyri scrolls. Another alternative is that Joseph received the Book of Abraham by revelation, like he did the Book of Moses. No one knows for sure where the Book of Abraham came from, but it came from somewhere. Truth seekers cannot ignore it. They must read it and seek to know whether it is true. This chapter does not solve the mystery of where exactly the Book of Abraham came from. It tells what the Book of Abraham restores and explains why it is so controversial.

The book is Abraham's autobiography, or at least the beginning of it. That does not mean that Abraham himself wrote it on the papyri Joseph Smith had. Ancient Near Eastern writings—including the ones in the Bible—were copied and recopied over and over before they came to us.

The Book of Abraham tells a harrowing tale. It starts with the understatement: "I, Abraham, saw that it was needful for me to obtain another place of residence" (Abraham 1:1). Translation: My apostate dad is trying to have me sacrificed to his gods. Abraham lived in Chaldea in what is now Syria or Turkey (maybe Iraq). He was a first-class seeker. He wanted to obtain greater knowledge, follow righteousness, and to receive instructions from God. More than anything, he wanted a family that would last forever. So he needed and sought to make covenants mediated by priesthood that could endow him with the power of godliness that could get him back to his Heavenly Father (see Doctrine and Covenants 84).

Just as Abraham was about to be sacrificed to the Egyptian gods that were worshipped in Chaldea at the time, the Lord answered his prayer, appeared to him in some way or another, and rescued him (see Abraham 1:15). God covenanted with Abraham that He would provide him a promised land and endow him with the power of priesthood covenants.

Abraham married Sarai, and they moved west toward the Mediterranean Sea. The Lord promised them endless posterity to "bear this . . . priesthood unto all nations" (Abraham 2:9). The Book of Abraham includes several revelations he received. It says the Lord gave him seer stones and that he learned through them how the universe works. Very importantly, the Lord showed him the premortal, pre-earth world inhabited by intelligences. God stood in the midst of the best and the brightest and chose them as leaders. He told Abraham that he was one of them.

Abraham said that the best of them all was like God himself, and He said to the others, "We will go down, for there is space there, and we will take of these materials, and we will make an earth whereon these [spirits] may dwell; and we will prove them . . . to see if they will do all things whatsoever the Lord their God shall command them" (Abraham 3:24–25).

Those whom God could trust to do whatever He commanded would get more power. God asked who He should send, and the one who was most like Him said, "Send me." Another one piped up and said, "Send me," and God said, "I will send the first." That made the second one angry (we learn from Doctrine and Covenants 29 and the Book of Moses that his motives were manipulative and evil), and he was cast out of heaven and took a bunch of God's children with him.

Abraham saw the creation process in his seer stones, and his account of it says clearly what the versions in Genesis and the Book of Moses obscure: that "the God*s* [plural], organized and formed the heavens and the earth" (Abraham 4:1; emphasis added). And instead of doing it in *days*, as the other accounts say, Abraham uses the word *time* to describe creative periods.

Abraham saw that the Gods created Adam and Eve and situated them in a spectacular garden, and then the story ends abruptly. It seems like Abraham had more to say, but we do not have it. Joseph Smith planned to publish more of it, but he was killed before he could.

How did we get the part of Abraham's autobiography we have? The verifiable facts are that in about 1820, an Italian explorer uncovered a tomb near Thebes, Egypt, containing mummies and papyri. Later, eleven of the mummies and some papyri (scrolls and other pieces) were sent to New York City. Michael Chandler then toured the country with these antiquities, selling them off in the process. In June 1835, he arrived in Kirtland, Ohio, with four mummies, two papyrus scrolls, and other ancient writings. William Phelps wrote to his wife that Joseph Smith said "that the rolls of papyrus contained a sacred record kept by Joseph in Pharaoh's court in Egypt and the teachings of Father Abraham."[1]

The Saints purchased the documents and mummies. Joseph's journal includes several entries in the fall of 1835 showing that he studied the Egyptian documents. John Whitmer testified, "Joseph the Seer saw these Record[s] and by the revelation of Jesus Christ could translate these records."[2] Warren Parrish said he scribed as Joseph translated Egyptian writing by revelation.[3] Joseph said in a sermon less than two weeks before his murder, "I learned . . . by translating the papyrus now in my house."[4]

The Book of Abraham was first published in the Church's newspaper early in 1842, including three facsimiles or copies of graphics along with explanations or interpretations.

Early in the spring of 1850, thirty-year-old apostle Franklin Richards arrived in Britain to lead more than 30,000 British Saints. He brought with him an idea for a new booklet of revelations that were not generally available. Published in 1851 as the Pearl of Great Price, the salmon-colored booklet included the Book of Abraham. At general conference in October 1880, the assembled Saints accepted the Pearl of Great Price—and the Book of Abraham—as scripture.

After Joseph was murdered, his mother kept the mummies and most of the Egyptian papyri in Illinois. Then, after she died, her daughter-in-law and Joseph's widow, Emma Hale Smith, sold these artifacts. The collection was later divided, and some of it ended up in a Chicago museum that burned in 1871. Some of it ended up in the Metropolitan Museum of Art in New York City, which transferred its papyrus fragments to The Church of Jesus Christ of Latter-day

Saints in 1967. Meanwhile, the Saints who followed Brigham Young preserved the Book of Abraham manuscripts as well as other documents from the 1830s. So now the Egyptian papyri that still exist and the Book of Abraham manuscripts and related papers are all together in the Church History Library in Salt Lake City. They are also online at josephsmithpapers.org.

When Joseph had possession of the Egyptian scrolls, no one in the United States could read them. Now that Egyptologists can read them, the scrolls Joseph once had are not available to read but some of the damaged fragments are. Whether they believe the Book of Abraham or not, everyone who is able to read these fragments agrees that the Book of Abraham is *not* on them. There is no agreement, however, on whether the Book of Abraham was written on papyri that is now lost.

In Nauvoo in February 1843, Lucy Mack Smith showed Charlotte Haven "a long roll of manuscript" and "heiroglyphics from another roll." Charlotte described them as depicting "Mother Eve being tempted by the serpent, who—the serpent I mean—was standing on the tip of his tail, which with his two legs formed a triangle, and had his head in Eve's ear."[5] This is important evidence to know about. It affirms that Joseph had a scroll and it included writings that are not on the pieces of papyri that still exist.

That verifiable fact should slow down our thinking and keep us from assuming too much. Both believers and unbelievers have made unproven assumptions about the Book of Abraham. Many Latter-day Saints assume (but do not know) that Abraham himself wrote on the papyri Joseph possessed. Respected Egyptologist Robert Ritner concluded that the Book of Abraham text is so tied to the facsimiles in the Book of Abraham, which he and others believe are not about Abraham, that the book cannot be true. This is what "Translation and Historicity of the Book of Abraham" is referring to when it says, "Some have assumed that the hieroglyphs adjacent to and surrounding facsimile 1 must be a source for the text of the book of Abraham. But this claim rests on the assumption that a vignette and its adjacent text must be associated in meaning. In fact, it was not uncommon for ancient Egyptian vignettes to be placed some distance from their associated commentary."[6]

There are three handwritten manuscripts of the Book of Abraham in the Church History Library in the handwriting of Warren Parrish, William Phelps, and Frederick Williams. They were written in the summer and fall of 1835. The Gospel Topics essay explains, "Some evidence suggests that Joseph studied the characters on the Egyptian papyri and attempted to learn the Egyptian language. His history reports that, in July 1835, he was 'continually engaged in translating an alphabet to the Book of Abraham, and arranging a grammar of the Egyptian language as practiced by the ancients.' This 'grammar,' as it was called, consisted of columns of hieroglyphic characters followed by English translations recorded in a large notebook by Joseph's scribe, William W. Phelps. Another manuscript, written by Joseph Smith and Oliver Cowdery, has Egyptian characters followed by explanations. The relationship of these documents to the book of Abraham is not fully understood. Neither the rules nor the translations in the grammar book correspond to those recognized by Egyptologists today."

Smart, informed people interpret these facts differently depending on their assumptions about how a bunch of documents relate to each other. These documents belong to a collection commonly called the Egyptian Language Documents (ELD), but it is important to know that they are not the papyri from Egypt that the Saints purchased in 1835. Rather, these are documents made by Saints in the 1830s. Some of the documents are copies of ancient Egyptian writing and drawings. Other documents appear, at a glance, to be an attempt to decode the Egyptian writing, with glyphs or symbols on the left and a name or pronunciation for each one stretching to the right, along with a definition. Other documents include text from the Book of Abraham and some symbols written in the left margin.

There are various, unverifiable ways to interpret the verifiable facts. One way is that Joseph tried to translate the ancient writing, failed, and told people it was the Book of Abraham, which obviously—to an Egyptologist—it is not. But another way to interpret them is that the Lord revealed the eternally consequential Book of Abraham to Joseph, and then he and/or others tried to figure out how the Egyptian writing corresponded to the English word, and mainly failed at that interesting but eternally inconsequential effort.

Scholars continue to study all the available evidence and propose new interpretations to account for it. The best one so far comes from scholars Michael MacKay and Daniel Belnap. They thought slowly about these documents and others. They recognized that the interpretations of these documents pose a false dilemma, an either/or that the evidence disrupts. So their interpretation accounts for more facts than any previous interpretation, including that the symbols on the documents are not all Egyptian, and the symbols do not all align as they should if Saints were trying to match up what the symbols mean with the Book of Abraham text.

The MacKay/Belnap thesis holds that Joseph Smith was frustrated by the poor power of his language to communicate all that God had shown him. Joseph desired a better way, a pure language capable of conveying what he knew by revelation. He tried to come up with one after he envisioned the heavenly glories in 1832. Later, this interpretation says, he incorporated the Book of Abraham and related documents into that project. MacKay and Belnap suggest that the Egyptian language documents "do not represent any direct translation efforts, or even explicit 'reverse engineering' of the Abrahamic text, but instead they appear to be an evolving attempt to incorporate the newly acquired Egyptian papyri into a nascent language system referred to as the pure language."[7]

I eagerly digest every new piece of evidence and interpretation regarding the origins of the Book of Abraham. But the story of how we got the Book of Abraham is nowhere near as important as the story *in* the Book of Abraham. Joseph did not leave us clear evidence of how he got the Book of Abraham. Rather, he left us the book itself and its news that "at the first organization in heaven we were all present and saw the Savior chosen and appointed, and the plan of salvation made and we sanctioned it."[8] Joseph taught what he learned about God and gods from "Abraham's record."[9] The Book of Abraham is another eyewitness record about who the Gods are, what They do and what They are like, who we are and where we came from, and how we fit into Their plan for our happiness by fitting into Their covenant with Abraham—that through him and all others who make and keep covenants, "all the families of the earth [will be] blessed, even with the blessings of the Gospel, which are the blessings of salvation, even of life eternal" (Abraham 2:11).

One way or another, that book came from God through Joseph Smith.

16.

How Restored Priesthood Keys Solve the Soteriological Problem

Douglas Davies is an Anglican priest and a scholar of religion, especially of the restored gospel. In one of his books he wrote, "Latter-day Saint theology is, above all else, a theology of death's conquest."[1] This chapter will help explain what he means.

Remember that in early January 1831, the Lord commanded the Saints to gather to Ohio and promised that He would endow them with power there (see Doctrine and Covenants 38). They gathered to Ohio. The Lord commanded them to build a house of God, assemble in it solemnly, and promised that He would come to them there if they did (see Doctrine and Covenants 88). When they dragged their feet, the Lord explained that they had "sinned a very grievous sin"—He said that part twice—"in that they are walking in darkness at noon-day" (Doctrine and Covenants 95:3–6). Then He said, "I gave unto you a commandment that you should build a house, in the which house I design to endow those whom I have chosen with power from on high" (Doctrine and Covenants 95:8). The Saints got to work building the Lord's house after that.

By midwinter 1836, it was nearly finished. It had been more than twelve years since Moroni appeared to Joseph and told him God would send Elijah to restore priesthood and renew everlasting covenant promises so the purpose of the creation would be fulfilled rather than frustrated at the Lord's Second Coming. Just weeks later, Joseph's oldest brother, Alvin, died painfully. It stung when the Presbyterian Reverend Benjamin Stockton all but said at the funeral that Alvin had gone to hell. But in 1836, Joseph did not know any better. He knew from the Book of Mormon that unaccountable infants who die are not damned, but as far as Joseph knew, Reverend Stockton was right about Alvin.

It had been four years since the Lord commanded the Saints to build a house of God and six since He promised them an endowment of power in Kirtland. They had been slow to understand and obey, but they had done it. An impoverished group of fallen mortals—who wanted to become saints through the Atonement of Christ, be endowed with His power, and have their hearts turned and relationships sealed—had built a house of God that rose from the high ground above the Chagrin River. And in the process they sanctified themselves, as the Lord commanded, so they could enter His presence in His house (see Doctrine and Covenants 88).

William Phelps explained in a letter to his wife Sally:

> Our meeting[s] will grow more and more solemn, and will continue till the great solemn assembly when the house is finished! We are preparing to make ourselves clean, by first cleansing our hearts, forsaking our sins, forgiving every body;

putting on clean decent clothes, by anointing our heads and by keeping all the commandments. As we come nearer to God we see our imperfections and nothingness plainer and plainer.[2]

On January 21, 1836, Joseph gathered in the westernmost room on the top floor of the temple with his counselor, his clerk, his father (the Church patriarch), and the two bishoprics. They came freshly bathed, symbolizing their efforts to repent. Joseph had done all he was commanded to do except to convene the solemn assembly, and that was scheduled for the first Sabbath of spring about two months from then. It was time for the Lord to restore more.

But how would the Lord teach Joseph what he did not know that he did not know? How would the Lord resolve a problem that had beset Christianity for at least a thousand years, a problem based on an unsound assumption the whole Christian world shared, including Joseph and the Latter-day Saints? The Lord showed Joseph a vision of the future—of heaven—and made sure he saw Alvin there. That made Joseph marvel and wonder how Alvin got past the flaming gates of God's kingdom. Then, having provoked the question, the Lord answered it.

Before we learn the answer, we need some background to help us learn how Christianity came to consign Alvin to hell in the first place. *Soteriology* is theology about salvation. Christianity's soteriological problem is based on three premises:

1. God loves all people and desires their salvation (see 1 Timothy 2:3–4).
2. Salvation comes to those who knowingly and willfully accept Jesus Christ as their Savior (see John 3:16).

3. Most people live and die without accepting Christ, or even knowing that they could or should.

The problem says that all three premises are true, but they can't be reconciled. Unrestored solutions have to dismiss one of the premises. Maybe God does not desire the salvation of all people. Or maybe Jesus saves people who do not knowingly and willfully accept Him.

Early Christians avoided this problem because they did not make the assumption that makes it a problem in the first place. They did not assume that death was a deadline that determined a person's salvation. Peter taught that Jesus Christ preached His gospel to the dead so they could be judged as justly as the living (see 1 Peter 3:18–20; 4:6). Paul taught that Christians could be baptized for the dead (see 1 Corinthians 15:29).

Jeffery Trumbower's book *Rescue for the Dead* traces the doctrine of redemption for the dead through Christian history. It shows that it was Augustine (AD 354–430), not Jesus or His apostles, who decided that death should be a deadline that determined a person's salvation. But Augustine's view prevailed in Christ's church—at least in the West.

Many medieval Christians continued to believe that after His death and before His Resurrection, Christ opened spirit prison. They called this event "the harrowing of hell," and they created a lot of art depicting it. My favorite images are the ones in which hell is an awful monster, and Christ causes it to cough up its captive dead (as in 2 Nephi 9).[3]

The Protestant reformers followed Augustine on this point. Then along came Joseph Smith. He was immersed in Protestant assumptions, but he was willing to hear from the Lord. He wanted to know what the Lord had to say. And what the Lord said to Joseph on January 21, 1836, is among the greatest good news He has ever revealed:

> All who have died without a knowledge of this gospel, who would have received it if they had been permitted to tarry, shall be heirs of the celestial kingdom of God; Also all that shall die henceforth without a knowledge of it, who would have received it with all their hearts, shall be heirs of that kingdom; For I, the Lord, will judge all men according to their works, according to the desires of their hearts. (Doctrine and Covenants 137:7–10)

It is a person's desire, not the timing of their death, that is the determinant of their salvation through Jesus Christ. He saves all who desire to be saved by Him once they know that good news. Which side of death a person is on when they learn of Christ and choose Him does not make a difference. By exposing the assumption that death determines salvation and restoring the truth in its stead, Jesus Christ resolved the soteriological problem for Joseph and for everyone else (see Doctrine and Covenants 137).[4] Joseph Smith's journal entry for January 21, 1836, is our source for this knowledge.

Two months later, Joseph was back in the temple. He and his counselors and clerks composed an inspired prayer for the solemn assembly set to convene the next day, March 27, 1836. He had never given a prayer like that before. He let the Spirit teach him what to pray for. The prayer they wrote is in Doctrine and Covenants 109. It begins by thanking God. Then it makes requests of Him in the name of Jesus Christ. It is based on the temple instructions Joseph received from the Lord four years earlier (see Doctrine and Covenants 88).

Joseph asked God to accept the temple on the terms He had given in that revelation, instructions the Saints tried hard to fulfill so they could obtain the promised blessing of entering the Lord's presence (see Doctrine and Covenants 88:68; 109:4–12). Joseph prayed that the Saints would become like their Heavenly Father by degrees of glory as they obeyed His laws and prepared to enter His presence.

Joseph prayed that the Saints, "armed" or endowed with priesthood power from the temple, could go to "the ends of the earth" with the "exceedingly great and glorious tidings" of the gospel to gather Israel (Doctrine and Covenants 109:22–23). He asked God to protect the Saints from their enemies (see verses 24–33). He asked for mercy upon the Saints and sealing of the anointing ordinances that many of the priesthood brethren had received in the weeks leading up to the solemn assembly.

Joseph asked for the gifts of the Spirit to be poured out as on the biblical day of Pentecost (see Acts 2:2–3). He asked the Lord to protect and empower the missionaries and postpone judgment until they had gathered the righteous. He prayed that God's will might be done "and not ours" (Doctrine and Covenants 109:44).

Joseph prayed for Zion—that the Saints would be delivered from the prophesied calamities. He asked God to remember the Saints who had been oppressed and driven from Jackson County, Missouri, and he prayed for their deliverance. He even asked for mercy "upon the wicked mob, who have driven thy people, that they may cease to spoil, that they may repent of their sins if repentance is to be found" (verse 50).

He prayed for mercy on all nations and political leaders, so that the principles of individual agency in the United States Constitution would be established forever. He prayed for "all the poor, the needy, and afflicted ones of the earth" (verse 55) and for an end to prejudices so that the missionaries "may gather out the righteous to build a holy city to thy name, as thou hast commanded them" (verse 58).

Joseph prayed for more stakes to facilitate the gathering and growth of Zion. He prayed for "all the scattered remnants of Israel, who have been driven to the ends of the earth, [to] come to a knowledge of the truth, believe in the Messiah, and be redeemed from oppression" (verse 67).

He prayed for himself, reminding the Lord of his sincere effort to keep covenants. He asked for mercy for his family. He prayed that Emma and their children "may be exalted in thy [God's] presence" (verse 69). That was the first time any of his revelations used the word "exalted" to refer to the fulness of salvation through temple blessings. Joseph prayed that his in-laws would be converted. He prayed for the First Presidency and their families, for all the Saints and their families, and for their sick and afflicted. He repeated his plea for "all the poor and meek of the earth," and for the glorious kingdom of God to fill the earth as prophesied (verses 68–74).

Joseph prayed a temple prayer that the Saints would rise in the First Resurrection with pure garments, "robes of righteousness," and "crowns of glory upon our heads" to "reap eternal joy" (verse 76). He repeated the petition, "hear us," three times, and asked God to accept the prayers and petitions and offerings of the Saints in building the house to His name (verse 78).

He prayed for grace to enable the saints to join the choirs surrounding God's throne in the heavenly temple "singing Hosanna to God and the Lamb" (verse 79). Then he concluded by asking the

Lord to "let these, thine anointed ones, be clothed with salvation, and thy saints shout aloud for joy. Amen, and Amen" (verse 80).

When Joseph and his brethren felt good about the prayer they had written, they sent it next door to the printing office, where it was set in type, inked, and printed for the solemn assembly the next day.

Early in the morning on March 27, 1836, Saints began to fill the pews of the first-floor chapel. Joseph and other leaders ushered them in for more than an hour. At nine o'clock, they had to start turning people away and close the doors, as every seat and aisle was full. Around 1,000 Saints were shoulder to shoulder, "waiting to hear the word of the Lord from the mouth of his servants."[5]

In the afternoon session, Joseph read the dedicatory prayer. He dedicated the first house of the Lord in the last dispensation and set the pattern for all subsequent solemn assemblies met for the same holy purposes. Joseph's temple prayer invited mortals, who occupy a polluted telestial planet where they cannot think of more than one thing at a time and generally only in finite terms, to receive power that will enable them to journey to the real world where God lives "enthroned, with glory, honor, power, majesty, might, dominion, truth, justice, judgment, mercy, and an infinity of fulness, from everlasting to everlasting" (verse 77).

The choir, seated in the four corners of the room, sang "The Spirit of God." Joseph asked the Saints if they accepted the dedication, and they all did. The sacrament was blessed and passed, and Joseph testified of his mission. Oliver Cowdery testified of the truth of the Book of Mormon. Frederick Williams testified that he had seen an angel of God during the dedicatory prayer. More testifying followed, and when it was over the Saints "ended with loud acclamations of Hosanna! Hosanna! Hosanna to God and the Lamb, Amen, Amen, and Amen! Three times."[6]

As the Saints funneled out of the building eight hours after arriving, they offered what they had, totaling $963—the value of about $26,000 today. However imperfectly, they had done as commanded. They had worked hard to become sanctified. They had built the Lord a house and had assembled solemnly in it. They expected God to keep His promise and endow them with power.

A week after dedicating the house of the Lord in Kirtland, Joseph attended meetings there, including an afternoon sacrament meeting. Jews were celebrating the Passover season. For Christians it was Easter Sunday, April 3, 1836. After the sacrament, Joseph Smith and Oliver Cowdery retreated behind the heavy curtains used to divide the room and prayed silently. Joseph's scribe captured what happened next in Joseph's journal entry for that day (see Doctrine and Covenants 110).[7] Jesus Christ appeared in His House as promised and endowed His Saints with powerful priesthood keys delivered by ministering angels. Those ministers included Elijah, as promised to Joseph almost thirteen years earlier (see Doctrine and Covenants 2).

Joseph now had the commission as well as priesthood permission to gather Israel from every nation. He could endow Saints with priesthood power and seal them together with the promise that they would conquer death with their relationships intact, making the creation purposeful rather than wasted. Enjoy this high point: "The Spirit of God like a fire is burning. . . . Angels are coming to visit the earth. The Lord is extending the Saints' understanding. . . . The knowledge and power of God are expanding."[8] But do not expect it to continue without opposition.

Within two years of the Savior's visit to His House, the Saints would be overcome by materialism and contention toward one another. Their faithfulness would be tested. Joseph's life would be threatened. Fellow servants and former friends would turn on him. Then, intensifying a plot in which the stakes were already eternal life or death, the Lord added a ticking clock. He told Joseph he could only count on five more years to finish restoring the broken covenant—five years to resolve two remaining priesthood problems. Joseph had five years to gather Israel so the Saints could be endowed with—and sealed by—priesthood power.[9]

17.

Harriet Brunson, Jane Neyman, and Baptism for the Dead

In the same revelation that told Joseph his days were numbered, the Lord told him to flee Ohio for Missouri with his family and all his faithful friends.[1] After a few months of fighting for the Saints' rights in Missouri, Joseph was unjustly jailed for nearly half a year, waiting for due process in a state where Latter-day Saints had learned to expect none. While Joseph was there, the Lord reassured him, "thy days are known, and thy years shall not be numbered less" (Doctrine and Covenants 122:9).

By the summer of 1840, a year and a half of Joseph's guaranteed five had ticked away. He had sent apostle missionaries to England to begin gathering Israel from there, but he had not performed a temple ordinance. He did not have a temple to perform one in. To make things worse, for the second consecutive summer, malaria had swept through the Saints in Nauvoo, Illinois, killing many.

As we have seen, unrestored Christianity has some theological problems, including that of who receives salvation. It is only a problem for those who make an assumption that early Christians did not make: that death is a deadline that determines a person's salvation. Peter did not assume that. He taught that Jesus Christ ministered to the imprisoned spirits of the dead so that they could be judged as if they were still alive (see 1 Peter 3:18–20; 4:6). Paul cited baptisms for the dead being practiced by the saints of his day as evidence that the dead would be resurrected (see 1 Corinthians 15:29).

By the end of the fifth century AD, however, Augustine had shaped Christianity based on the assumption that there was no progress after death for those who had not been baptized before they died. A thousand years later, Martin Luther validated that assumption. So did John Calvin. It continues in much of unrestored Christianity, but the Savior who ministered to the spirits in prison between the time of His death and Resurrection revealed a solution to the soteriological problem that highlights how mighty He is to save.

Joseph's January 21, 1836, revelation (now known as Doctrine and Covenants 137) taught him that what a free agent desires to do with the Savior's Atonement once they know about it is what determines salvation. Death does not matter much. It does not change our desires nor disqualify us from choosing redemption through Christ. That knowledge was extremely consoling to the early Latter-day Saints, nearly all of whom had lost loved ones to death, and who had largely converted from Protestant Christianity. For evidence of that consolation, consider the funeral of Seymour Brunson: It's August 18, 1840, and sweltering outside in Nauvoo, Illinois. Joseph announced just a few weeks ago that he would build a temple there if the Saints would back him, and he prayed that the Lord would keep him alive long enough to see it. A large congregation has assembled in the grove where the largest Church meetings are held.

Joseph preaches the sermon for Seymour's wife, Harriet. Seymour was a good soul, faithful to his covenants. He has gone to rest. But what consoles Harriet could not console Jane Neyman, another woman in the crowd. She has a different problem. Her son Cyrus was old enough to be accountable for his sins when he died recently, and he was not baptized. Joseph sees Jane and knows how heavy her heart is. He had the same fears and worries until the Lord showed him his older brother Alvin in the celestial world. Joseph wants Jane to see that vision, so he opens the Bible and reads from Paul's first letter to the Corinthian Saints, which takes for granted that Christians perform proxy baptisms for people who died before they could be baptized themselves.

Joseph teaches that the Saints can and should follow that practice. According to one witness, Joseph said the Saints "could now act for their friends who had departed this life, and that the plan of salvation was calculated to save all who were willing to obey the requirements of the law of God."[2]

Here is the solution to the soteriological problem. It overturns the assumption that death is a deadline. The other premises of the problem are all true: God is powerful and loving. Salvation is in Christ, and the willful acceptance of that truth is necessary to be saved from sin (or else some may be saved against their will). And many, if not most, of God's children live and die without knowing that Jesus Christ can and will save them, but so what? Dying without that knowledge only matters if God is not the powerful, planning, equal-opportunity exalter that the Restoration reveals Him to be. Jane Neyman was thrilled by this restored truth. She asked Harvey Olmstead to baptize her in the Mississippi River for Cyrus on September 13, 1840. Vienna Jaques witnessed the ordinance from the back of her horse. When Joseph heard about it, he asked what Harvey had said and confirmed the ordinance had been done correctly.

If we think too fast, we might assume that is not how baptism for the dead works. We would be assuming either that Joseph knew more than he did, or that we know more than we do, or both. If so, we can choose to slow down, cut out the mental shortcuts, and evaluate the sources of our knowledge. We could then recognize that revelation comes in events like Joseph's vision on January 21, 1836, of Alvin in the celestial kingdom, or his sermon on August 18, 1840, at Brother Brunson's funeral. But it also required more revelation to fully understand those revelations. Joseph claimed to receive the Restoration by revelation a bit at a time. He did not know it all when he was fourteen or seventeen or twenty-four or thirty-four. He acted on what had been revealed to him and sought more and more and more. That is true, too, for the prophets who have succeeded him.

Joseph Smith Sr. died on September 14, 1840, just a day after Jane was baptized for Cyrus. Before he died, Joseph taught him baptism for the dead, and Joseph Sr. pled for his sons to ensure Alvin was baptized. As Joseph learned more about baptism for the dead, he gave it to the Saints. On December 15, 1840, he dictated a letter and sent it to the apostles who were on missions in Great Britain. The letter only occupies one and a half sheets of paper, but still contains six pages of text. It was written by Robert Thompson, who wrote horizontally on the front and back of a sheet and then the front of another sheet. Then he turned the paper ninety degrees and wrote three more pages across what he had already written. Then he folded it up, addressed it "To the Twelve," and sent it across the Atlantic Ocean.

"I presume," Joseph says in the letter, "the doctrine of 'baptism for the dead,' has ere this reached your ears, and may have raised some inquiries in your minds, respecting the same." The apostles' wives had indeed written the news to them almost immediately after Joseph revealed it. Joseph told them how he revealed it, relying on the Bible at Brother Brunson's funeral, and saying he had "since then given general instructions to the Church on the subject. The Saints have the privilege of being baptized for those of their relatives who are dead, who they believe would have embraced the gospel, if they had been privileged with hearing it, and who have received the gospel in the Spirit, through the instrumentality of those who have been commissioned to preach to them while in prison." Joseph thought the apostles would share his delight at the Lord's solution to the soteriological problem: "You will undoubtedly see its consistency and reasonableness and it presents the Gospel of Christ in probably a more enlarged scale than some have imagined it."[3]

A month later the Lord revealed to Joseph (and Joseph to the Saints) the vital need they had to finish building the temple in Nauvoo: "For a baptismal font there is not upon the earth, that they, my saints, may be baptized for those who are dead—for this ordinance belongeth to my house, and cannot be acceptable to me, only in the days of your poverty, wherein ye are not able to build a house unto me" (Doctrine and Covenants 124:29–30; see also verses 31–34). Joseph said the Lord would not always authorize the Saints to perform the ordinance outside the temple. They were baptized for the dead in the Mississippi River until October 3, 1841, and worked to prepare the temple font, where they started doing the ordinance well before the rest of the temple was finished. They were thrilled with the doctrine and what it said about God's love and what it promised about redemption for loved ones. Sarah Cleveland was baptized for forty friends and relatives. Nehemiah Brush was baptized for more than a hundred. Joseph immersed Saints for their ancestors more than 200 times.

In August 1842, Joseph taught the Relief Society sisters that "all persons baptized for the dead must have a recorder present, that he may be an eyewitness to testify of it."[4] The next day he wrote the letter in Doctrine and Covenants 127, including a revelation to the Saints to make sure their baptisms for the dead were witnessed and recorded on earth because that was a key to their being recorded in heaven. The Lord added, "I am about to restore many things to the Earth, pertaining to the Priesthood saith the Lord of Hosts."[5]

A week later Joseph wrote again, elaborating on the doctrine and practice of sealing and recording ordinances on earth and in heaven (see Doctrine and Covenants 128).

Brigham Young taught about this process of revelation:

> When an infinite being gives a law to his finite creatures, he has to descend to the capacity of those who receive his law, when the doctrine of baptism for the dead was first given, this church was in its infancy. . . . The Lord has led this people all the while in this way, by giving them here a little and there a little, thus he increases their wisdom, and he that receives a little and is thankful for that shall receive more.

President Young explained further:

> Joseph in his life time did not receive every thing connected with the doctrine of redemption, but he has left the key with those who understand how to obtain and teach to this great people all that is necessary for their salvation and exaltation in the celestial kingdom of our God.[6]

DISPENSING FULNESS

18.

Relief Society, Masonry, and the Endowment of Power

This chapter tells how the Lord restored the temple endowment through Joseph Smith, and how He prepared sisters for it via Relief Society and brothers via Masonry.

Sarah Melissa Granger Kimball was in her early twenties on March 17, 1842, and she lived in Nauvoo. Her comfortable, white frame home stood about a mile from Joseph Smith's store, behind which the Mississippi River made a big bend and passed down the road, out to her home.

Up the hill in the other direction the walls of the temple were rising, and Sarah wanted to do her part to finish the temple. So she and several of her Latter-day Saint sisters met in her home, where Sarah and seamstress Margaret Cook explained their desire to form a relief society for the impoverished people working on the temple—many of them new converts and British immigrants. Women everywhere were forming relief societies for good causes. Sarah and her sisters delegated Eliza Snow to write down their society's purpose and principles, as all good relief societies did.

Eliza took notes and then visited Joseph to read her document to him. He said it was better than any like it. "But," he said, "this is not what you want. Tell the sisters their offering is accepted of the Lord and he has something better for them." Inviting the group to gather the next Thursday afternoon in the spacious second-story room above his store, he promised, "I will organize the women under the priesthood after the pattern of the priesthood."[1]

The night before Sarah and her sisters climbed the stairs to the second floor of Joseph's store, Heber Kimball and others came down those same stairs after a jam-packed two days. Abraham Jonas had been in town. He was a Jew from Jacksonville, Illinois, and grand master of all the Masons in the state. He had just installed a Masonic Lodge and inducted new members, and on March 15, 1842, he let Joseph Smith enter the lodge as an apprentice and passed him as a fellow. Then, on March 16, he raised Joseph Smith as a Master Mason.

What does that mean? We have to go back in time even further to learn what it meant to Heber Kimball. He was four years older than Joseph Smith and had been one of the apostles since 1835. He had recently returned from his second mission to England. Twenty years earlier, before the Savior restored His church, Heber married Vilate Murray and they both longed for an endowment of divine power—something that would give meaning and direction to their lives and make sense of the world as it was and relate it to the world to come. Vilate bore a daughter, Helen, in 1823. She and Heber bought land and built a fine house, a woodshed, and a barn. They planted an orchard and were living comfortably, at least physically.

Then tuberculosis stole Heber's mother in 1824, his father a year later, and his brother and sister-in-law a year after that. No house, no matter how well-built, nor any amount of property, could endow Heber Kimball with power over death and restore the relationships it had severed. Death could snatch Heber or Vilate or their daughter at any instant, and Heber wanted richer relationships, more meaning, more security, and more power than hard work alone could offer.[2]

So even though Heber was a potter and a blacksmith, he became a Mason—not a bricklaying mason, but a member of the Masonic fraternity. He and fellow Masons held elaborate meetings where they retold stories of the ancient origins of the masons Solomon commissioned to build the temple in Jerusalem. These stories taught Heber to be loyal and trustworthy.[3] Masons in western New York where Heber lived held their meetings in a tavern room representing Solomon's temple. In their meetings, Masons acted out and enlarged the brief biblical account of Hiram of Tyre, a widow's son of the tribe of Naphtali (see 1 Kings 7). They used symbols, including the pillars of Solomon's temple, the sun, moon, and stars, the compass, square, and the all-seeing eye.

In the Masonic story, Solomon charges Hiram to build the temple. Hiram refuses to reveal the word of the Master Mason to some of his subordinates, and they murder him for his fidelity and integrity. Emulating Hiram, Masons ritually advanced by degrees from Entered Apprentice to Fellow Craft to Master Mason, using gestures, secret words, and ritual clothing.

The Masons let Heber enter their lodge as an apprentice in a ceremony.[4] With each meeting, he learned various signs, words, and symbols he promised not to reveal, all of which conveyed that he was building on a solid foundation and adding to it by degrees of light and knowledge through symbolic ritual. As Heber advanced in the order, he metaphorically went deeper into Solomon's temple on a quest for more light, rising to the degree of a Fellow Craft, then finally becoming a Master Mason.

But that's as far as the young Heber went with Masonry, for just as he was about to go further, a Mason named William Morgan, who was publishing Masonic secrets in a nearby town, disappeared and was never heard from again. Many people suspected Masons of capturing and executing Morgan, so a great outcry against Masonry followed. In the aftermath of Morgan's disappearance, the popularity of Masonry plummeted in the region and Heber's involvement waned. It was a loss to Heber, who had enjoyed the ideals and friendships Masonry provided and the feeling of growth he experienced within the group.[5] The rituals and stories they shared and discussed made Heber and his fellow Masons feel like they were part of something ancient and mysterious.

Then Heber found something better. He found the restored gospel of Jesus Christ. So did fellow masons Newel Whitney, Hyrum Smith, and others. By March 1842, the anti-masonic feelings had moderated enough for them to start a Masonic lodge in Nauvoo, and Joseph Smith had joined it.[6] Heber and some others who were present noted the events in their journals, but at the time no one, including Joseph, documented why he joined or what he thought about the Masonic stories and rituals.[7]

On Thursday, March 17, 1842, at a few minutes before one o'clock, Emma crossed the muddy street, climbed the stairs, and took a seat with nineteen other women—her sisters in the faith, some of her dearest friends—in the room above the store. A Bible lay open in the room, left from the previous evening's Masonic meeting, and with it a scrap of paper on which someone had written a prayer that would have been as heartfelt to the sisters as it was to the Masons. "O, Lord," it said, "help our widows and fatherless children."[8]

Joseph Smith had come too, as well as apostles Willard Richards and John Taylor, whose wife Leonora played the small organ. Half the women were single, half married. Two were widowed, including Philindia Myrick, whose husband had been murdered in Missouri. Three of the sisters were teenagers. Sarah Cleveland, in her fifties, was the oldest. Poetess Eliza Snow sat alongside less educated sisters. Fortunate, prosperous Sarah Kimball sat alongside poorer sisters who possessed little more than the dresses they wore.

Joseph invited the sisters to nominate a president who would then nominate counselors. Emma was the sisters' unanimous choice for their president. When discerning who her counselors should be, Emma chose two women who had housed her family when they were homeless. When Emma first arrived in Kirtland, poor, pregnant, and cold in the early days of 1831, it was Elizabeth Ann Whitney who invited her and Joseph to stay in her home. Later, during another homeless period, Elizabeth Ann provided Emma the apartment above the Whitney store. There Emma gave birth to her son Joseph III in 1832. And Sarah Cleveland had done similar service for Emma and her four children during that terrible winter when they were exiled from Missouri. That was before Sarah was a Latter-day Saint.

In organizing the sisters "after the pattern of the priesthood," Joseph was preparing them for the temple endowment and sealing ordinances. He spoke in subsequent Relief Society meetings, referring regularly to the promised blessings of the temple endowment and encouraging the sisters to prepare for them.[9] He wanted them to understand that God intended to endow them with priesthood power. He had learned a decade earlier that the power to regain God's presence and abide there could only be obtained through temple covenants and ordinances (see Doctrine and Covenants 84). He promised the Relief Society sisters the same temple ordinances the men would receive and said that if they were faithful to their covenants they would "come into the presence of God."

He taught them "that the church is not now organiz'd in its proper order, and cannot be until the Temple is completed."[10] The loftiness of Joseph's teachings clashed with a grim prophecy he made and Eliza Snow recorded in the minutes: "He did not know as he should have many opportunities of teaching them—that they were going to be left to themselves,—they would not long have him to instruct them— that the church would not have his instruction long, and the world would not be troubled with him a great while, and would not have his teachings— He spoke of delivering the keys to this Society and to the church—that according to his prayers God had appointed him elsewhere."[11] Joseph's journal entry for the day says he "gave a lecture on the priesthood showing how the sisters would come in possession of the privileges and blessings and gifts of the priesthood," meaning the endowment of power and sealing ordinances.[12]

A week later, Joseph called on a Mason named Lucius Scovill to transform the rooms above his store into a temporary temple. The next day, May 4, 1842, Joseph gathered his brother Hyrum and a few other trusted associates including Brigham Young, Heber Kimball, and Newell Whitney into the sacred space. There he gave them the endowment of power. His history says he spent the day on the upper floor of the store, where he "kept [his] sacred writings, translated ancient records, and received revelations" and where the Masons met. Joseph instructed them in the principles and order of the Priesthood, attending to washings, anointings, endowments and the communication of Keys pertaining to the Aaronic Priesthood, and so on to the highest order of Melchisedec Priesthood, setting forth . . . all those plans and principles, by which any one is enabled to secure the fulness of those blessings, which have been prepared for the Church of the first born, and come up and abide in the presence of the Eloheim in the Eternal worlds. In this Council was instituted the Ancient order of things for the first time in these last days. And the communications I made to this Council were of things Spiritual, and to be received only by the Spiritual minded: and there was nothing made known to these men, but what will be made known to all <the> Saints of the last days, so soon as they are prepared to receive, and a proper place is prepared to communicate them, even to the weakest of the Saints. therefore let the Saints be diligent in building the Temple, and all houses which they have been, or shall hereafter be commanded of God to build; and wait their time with patience, in all meekness, faith and perserverance unto the end, knowing assuredly that all these things referred to, in this Counsel, are always governed by the principle of Revelation.[13]

Each of the men Joseph endowed that day was a Master Mason. Most of them had participated in Masonic meetings in the same space, which also represented a temple. As Masons, they learned through rituals how to increase in knowledge and serve their fellow Masons. Through the endowment, they learned through similar rituals as they covenanted with God to keep the laws governing their return to His presence. Joseph picked these men specifically, maybe in part because they were Masons, and began teaching in a way they understood, starting where they were and leading them to more light and knowledge.

After he received the priesthood endowment from Joseph Smith, Heber Kimball wrote to his fellow apostle Parley Pratt, who was still preaching in England: "We have received some pressious things through the Prophet on the preasthood that would caus your Soul to rejoice. . . . I can not give them to you on paper for they are not to be riten. So you must come and get them for your Self." Heber also told Parley, "We have organized a Lodge here of Masons," adding that Joseph Smith and most of the apostles were among more than 200 men who had joined. "Thare is a similarity of preast Hood in masonry," he explained. "Br. Joseph ses masonry was taken from priesthood but has become degenerated. But menny things are perfect."[14]

Today you can find numerous sites claiming that Joseph Smith simply stole the temple endowment from Masonry. The first person to make that charge was John C. Bennett, who did not know the content of the temple endowment for himself, and who had been grinding a bitter ax against Joseph since the Church excommunicated him for his predatory sexual abuse of several women. Bennett had been a Mason but was expelled from more than one lodge for his bad behavior.

Heber Kimball, on the other hand, was perfectly positioned to know whether the endowment was microwaved Masonry or something better. He testified that it was something better. Similar? Obviously. Overlap in symbols? Definitely. But not the same meaning, and not even close to the same purpose or power or priesthood. Masons covenant with each other to be good men. Saints covenant with God to obey His laws so they can advance by degrees of glory back into His presence.[15]

Three weeks after Joseph first gave the endowment, the Relief Society met in the grove near the rising temple, having long since outgrown the room above Joseph's store. Emma opened the meeting and welcomed 187 new sisters into the Society. She coordinated their service projects and then invited her husband to the stand along with Bishop Newel K. Whitney, who was the husband of her counselor, Elizabeth Ann Whitney. Emma then invited Bishop Whitney to speak. Remember that he had received his endowment from Joseph three weeks earlier.

Bishop Whitney understood the Prophet's vision, and he spoke about preparing "for those blessings which God is soon to bestow upon us." He went right to the heart of the temple blessings. "In the beginning," he said, "God created man male and female and bestow'd upon man certain blessings peculiar to a man of God, of which woman partook, so that without the female all things cannot be restor'd to the earth it takes all to restore the Priesthood." Joseph had nothing to add to the bishop's inspired teachings on temple preparation.[16]

President Russell M. Nelson has taught similarly:

> Every woman and every man who makes covenants with God and keeps those covenants, and who participates worthily in priesthood ordinances, has direct access to the power of God. Those who are endowed in the house of the Lord receive a gift of God's priesthood power by virtue of their covenant, along with a gift of knowledge to know how to draw upon that power.

> The heavens are just as open to *women* who are endowed with God's power flowing from their priesthood covenants as they are to men who bear the priesthood. I pray that truth will register upon each of your hearts because I believe it will change your life. Sisters, you have the right to draw liberally upon the Savior's power to help your family and others you love.[17]

With little time remaining to finish his mission of solving the remaining priesthood problems by endowing and sealing the Saints, Joseph Smith tapped into the established institutions of relief societies and Masonic lodges, filled them with revelation, adapted them to God's purposes, and made them something better. That is how the Restoration resolved one of the two remaining priesthood problems: namely that without the ordinances and covenants of Melchizedek priesthood, no one can be endowed with the power needed to regain God's presence and remain there (see Doctrine and Covenants 84:19–23).

19.

Melissa and Benjamin Johnson Learn the New and Everlasting Covenant

Death defeats marriage. So do a lot of other powerful forces. But in the divine plan of our heavenly parents, our marriages are meant to last as long as theirs does. This chapter highlights the terms, conditions, and eternal importance of the new and everlasting covenant of marriage and tells how it was restored.

A common marriage ceremony in unrestored Christianity unites a wife and husband "as long as we both shall live," or "till death do us part." None of the churches could marry a couple longer than that even though people everywhere longed for a forever family. In 1840, only Joseph Smith had been empowered and commissioned by God to seal families forever.

Hoping a marriage will last forever, or wishing it to be so, or even writing vows that say so, does not make it so. Marriage can last forever, but only in the new and everlasting covenant, according to the Lord (see Doctrine and Covenants 132:7 and 132:19–20). The challenge of that text is that knowing what it says is not the same as knowing what it means.

As best we can tell, Joseph Smith began teaching at least some things about the new and everlasting covenant of marriage in the mid-1830s. That is when William Phelps wrote to his wife in Missouri about what he learned from Joseph in Ohio: "A new idea Sally, if you and I continue faithful to the end, we are certain to be one in the Lord throughout eternity; this is one of the most glorious consolations we can have in the flesh."[1]

A few years later, Joseph taught Parley Pratt "great and glorious principles concerning God and the heavenly order of eternity." Parley wrote later that Joseph taught him that marriage could be "for time and all eternity; and that the refined sympathies and affections which endeared us to each other emanated from the fountain of divine eternal love. It was from him that I learned that we might cultivate these affections, and grow and increase in the same to all eternity; while the result of our endless union would be an offspring as numerous as the stars of heaven, or the sands of the sea shore." That truth made all the difference to Parley, who concluded, "I had loved before, but I knew not why. But now I loved—with a pureness—an intensity of elevated, exalted feeling, which would lift my soul from the transitory things of this groveling sphere and expand it as the ocean. . . . In short, I could now love with the spirit and with the understanding also."[2]

Let's review how Joseph came to know and teach this truth, this new and everlasting covenant of marriage. It was 1823 when Moroni appeared and explained that Elijah would be sent to Joseph with priesthood that could seal families, and that if it did not take hold before the Savior's Second Coming, the creation would go to waste (see Doctrine and Covenants 2). Thirteen years later, Elijah conferred keys of the priesthood on Joseph (see Doctrine and Covenants 110).

Now imagine that it is May 16, 1843. It has been more than five years since Joseph confided to friends the Lord's promise to keep him alive for at least five more years. Joseph is in a hurry. He is in the home of friends Melissa and Benjamin Johnson, who were married two years earlier on Christmas and have one child so far.

This is Benjamin's memory of what happened: "In the evening [Joseph] called me and my wife to come and sit down, for he wished to marry us according to the Law of the Lord. I thought it a joke, and said I should not marry my wife again, unless she courted me, for I did it all the first time. He chided my levity, told me he was in earnest, and so it proved, for we stood up and were sealed by the Holy Spirit of Promise."[3]

Then, with Melissa and Ben's undivided attention, Joseph taught them the terms and conditions of the covenant they had just made—the new and everlasting covenant of marriage. Joseph's clerk and recorder, William Clayton, was with him. He recorded part of what Joseph said:

> . . . in order to obtain the highest [degree of glory] a man [and woman] must enter into this order of the priesthood and if he dont he cant obtain it. He may enter into the other but that is the end of his kingdom he cannot have an increase.

Joseph taught that only the highest glory—what we call exaltation—includes the power to create life eternally:

> He said that except a man and his wife enter into an everlasting covenant and be married for eternity while in this probation by the power and authority of the Holy priesthood

they will cease to increase when they die (ie. they will not have any children in the resurrection, but those who are married by the power & authority of the priesthood in this life & continue [to keep their covenants] without committing the sin against the Holy Ghost will continue to increase & have children in the celestial glory.

Then, to explain what Doctrine and Covenants 132:7 describes as "that too most holy," Joseph put his hand on William Clayton's knee and used him as an example. "He is sealed up by the power of the priesthood unto eternal life," Joseph explained, "having taken the step which is necessary for that purpose."

When Joseph visited, taught, and sealed Melissa and Ben Johnson, the terms and conditions of the new and everlasting covenant of marriage were not yet written down. Nor had the covenant been taught specifically to the Saints generally. William Clayton's journal says that Joseph was picking and choosing a few couples to seal: "said that the way he knew in whom to confide, God told him in whom he might place confidence."[4]

The new and everlasting covenant of marriage was finally recorded a few months later. Joseph's July 12, 1843, journal entry reports that he received a revelation in the presence of his brother Hyrum and William Clayton. That revelation, Doctrine and Covenants 132, sets the terms and conditions of exaltation through the new and everlasting covenant of marriage. Verses 1–28 repeatedly set forth three steps to making and keeping the new and everlasting covenant of marriage. It is a challenging text, perhaps by divine design, but we can decode it when we know what Joseph Smith was teaching and doing (and assigning others to do) in connection with it.

In August 1843, Joseph taught the Saints about "the power of endless life." We have a few versions of incomplete notes of what he said. The notes by Willard Richards in Joseph's journal tell us that he talked about priesthood and holding keys of power and blessings including "kingly powers of anointing." Joseph taught that "salvation could not come into the world without the mediation of Jesus Christ." He asked, "How shall God come to the rescue of this generation?" Then answered, "He shall send Elijah . . . and he shall reveal the covenants to seal." Then Williard's notes say, "called elected and made sure," and include the later insertion just before that, "anointing and sealing." Toward the end of his remarks, according to Willard's notes, Joseph said, "Finish that temple, and God will fill it with power."[5]

William Clayton's notes make it clearer that Joseph was speaking about Hebrews 7–8, which is about Melchizedek being a king and a priest of the Most High God (see Hebrews 7:1, NRSV). Then it becomes about Jesus Christ as *the* Melchizedek, the King and Priest forever. "Accordingly Jesus has also become the guarantor of a better covenant" (Hebrews 7:22, NRSV).[6] In the notes James Burgess made, Joseph asked, "What was the design of the almighty in making man, it was to exalt him to be as God." That, Joseph said, was "the mystery and power and glory of the priesthood." He called it "so great and glorious."[7]

According to Burgess, Joseph referred repeatedly to the "fulness of the priesthood." The scriptures use that word *fulness* to describe the richness of the restoration generally. But the scriptures also mean something more specific when they use the word *fulness* as Joseph did. This is demonstrated by Doctrine and Covenants 132:6, in which the word is used twice. It says that "the new and everlasting covenant . . . was instituted for the fulness of my glory; and he that receiveth a fulness thereof must and shall abide the law" (Doctrine and Covenants 132:6). To grasp what the Savior means by "fulness of my glory," we need to review what he had taught Joseph over the years. It is that priesthood—not office, mind you, but power, God's power—holds the key to knowing God and to knowing what God knows (see Doctrine and Covenants 84:19). That power is manifested in the ordinances of the priesthood. So "without the ordinances . . . of the priesthood . . . the power" is not manifested to us, and without an endowment of this power, no one can regain God's presence and stay there (see Doctrine and Covenants 84:19–24).

Being endowed with God's power is key to the knowledge of God. The Lord's revelations to Joseph equate that power with *light, law, life, truth, glory,* and *intelligence* (see Doctrine and Covenants 88 and 93). To grasp this concept, we will need to understand what the Lord means by these words. So here is a bit of what He says about them: Light proceeds from His presence and fills the immensity of space. This substance is what gives life, and it's also "the law by which all things are governed," and also "the power of God" (Doctrine and Covenants 88:11–14). It is also the glory of God. And the glory of God is the same as intelligence, or, coming full circle, light. And light is truth (see Doctrine and Covenants 93:36). Indeed, "truth shineth," the Lord told Joseph (Doctrine and Covenants 88:7).

This marvelous substance—truth, light, law, life, glory, power, intelligence—has fascinating properties. It is limitless, for one. It is accumulated not in a lab or a library but by *receiving* it from God, who gives it to all who receive it. The scriptures associate keeping God's commandments with receiving this power. That's the same as obeying His laws, receiving His light, being endowed with His power. You get the idea. Anyone who keeps "commandments receiveth truth and light, until [they are] glorified in truth and knoweth all things" (Doctrine and Covenants 93:28).

We get to take as much of this substance as we accumulate here with us when we die. Joseph revealed that the "intelligence we attain unto in this life . . . will rise with us in the resurrection" (Doctrine and Covenants 130:18). And in that same passage we see again how to acquire and accumulate this substance: it cleaves to people who diligently obey laws that were irrevocably decreed in heaven before the foundations of this world. This most wonderful of all substances can also be taken away. But the revelations do not say that God takes it away. They say, "that wicked one cometh and taketh away light and truth, through disobedience, from the children of men, and because of the tradition of their fathers" (Doctrine and Covenants 93:39). The revelations equate accumulating light with knowledge and knowing, and they equate that kind of knowing with worship. In other words, we worship a God who has all of this glory. And we worship Him by becoming like Him (obtaining glory). And we obtain glory the way Jesus did.

Jesus did not start with all of God's glory (or what the revelations call fulness). He obtained it one degree at a time. Or in other words, He went from "grace to grace, until he received a fulness" (Doctrine and Covenants 93:13). By Him and in Him and through Him, we can do the same. As the Savior put it, "if you keep my commandments you shall receive of his fulness, and be glorified in me as I am in the Father" (Doctrine and Covenants 93:20). All that leads to the new and everlasting covenant of marriage: the law that leads to exaltation, or the fulness of God's glory. In Doctrine and

Covenants 132:7, the Lord reveals the conditions that lead to exaltation.

1. Making the new and everlasting covenant of marriage
2. Having the covenant sealed by the Holy Spirit of Promise
3. Receiving that most holy

Joseph and Emma made the new and everlasting covenant of marriage in May 1843. They were sealed by the Holy Spirit of Promise, "which the Father sheds forth upon all those who are just and true"—all, in other words, who keep their covenants (Doctrine and Covenants 76:53).

The sealing of the Holy Spirit of Promise guarantees the new and everlasting covenant. The Holy Spirit of Promise withdraws His seal when covenanters are not just and true. Being just and true means being faithful to the covenant in the same sense as spouses vow to be faithful to each other. In the new and everlasting covenant of marriage, spouses covenant not only to cleave to each other, but to God. Every blessing sealed upon their heads is conditioned entirely upon this faithfulness. Faithfulness is not flawlessness—it is total devotion to God and to one's spouse. It means no other gods get in the way. No other gods have power to fulfill the promises of priesthood power for themselves and their endless posterity, protection from enemies, and a promised land hereafter.

Joseph's journal entry for September 28, 1843, records a meeting of the Saints who had received the endowment and sealing ordinances. That day, Joseph and Emma received what Joseph's journal calls the "highest and holiest order of the priesthood"—the ordinance Doctrine and Covenants 132:7 calls "that too most holy." Then they had what Joseph called "fulness of the priesthood," and fulness of God's glory is the purpose of the new and everlasting covenant.[8]

I recognize that this can be quite confusing. I think it is intentionally esoteric. It is hidden in plain sight to be accessible to seekers who want to understand the new and everlasting covenant with real intent, a sincere heart, and faith in Jesus Christ. As if the Lord knows all that best of all, he restates the terms of the covenant in Doctrine and Covenants 132:19–20. As you read that passage slowly, notice that the words between the dashes correspond to what verse 7 called "that too most holy" and what Joseph's journal calls the "highest and holiest order of the priesthood"—what he referred to as the fulness of the priesthood. As you read verse 19, pay particular attention to the if/then sequence. The *if* has three parts, connected to each other by the word *and*. That all leads to the second dash, which is followed by the *then*—the most spectacular *then* possible. Think slowly:

> And again, verily I say unto you, *if* a man marry a wife by my word, which is my law, and by the new and everlasting covenant, *and* it is sealed unto them by the Holy Spirit of promise, by him who is anointed, unto whom I have appointed this power and the keys of this priesthood; *and* it shall be said unto them—Ye shall come forth in the first resurrection; and if it be after the first resurrection, in the next resurrection; and shall inherit thrones, kingdoms, principalities, and powers, dominions, all heights and depths. . . . *Then shall they be gods*, because they have no end; therefore shall they be from everlasting to everlasting, because they continue; then shall they be above all, because all things are subject unto them. Then shall they be gods, because

they have all power, and the angels are subject unto them. (Doctrine and Covenants 132:19–20; emphasis added)

Joseph Smith gave the highest, holiest ordinances of the priesthood to Mary Ann and Brigham Young on November 22, 1843. Then Joseph instructed Brigham to give them to most of the apostles and their wives.[9] Wilford Woodruff's journal documents how Brigham Young fulfilled his assignment.[10] This is what Joseph was teaching Melissa and Ben Johnson to live for, prepare for, and anticipate when he told them that William Clayton had been "sealed up by the power of the priesthood unto eternal life having taken *the step which is necessary for that purpose.*"[11]

Because of Jesus Christ, the new and everlasting covenant of marriage defeats death and every other disruptive force for as long as the marriage remains sealed by the Holy Spirit of Promise. Everyone who wants to make and keep the new and everlasting covenant of marriage and receive the blessings of exaltation will be able to do so. As the Lord has declared and as Joseph Smith and his successors have taught, there is a plan of happiness for everyone who chooses it. Everyone who chooses to make and keep covenants to live the laws of God accumulates light, life, truth, law, glory, power, and intelligence. They are, in other words, endowed with power. God's power. Everyone who makes and keeps the new and everlasting covenant of marriage, whether here or hereafter, becomes like their heavenly parents.

20.

How Joseph Smith Tasked Brigham Young to Carry On the Restoration

The temple is progressing well at the present time," Wilford Woodruff wrote in his journal in 1842, but the progress was not fast enough for Joseph Smith.[1] He was thirty-seven years old, and he knew he would not live to be forty.[2] So on May 3, 1842, Joseph turned the rooms on the second floor above his store into a temporary temple. The next day, Joseph gathered his brother Hyrum, Newel K. Whitney, apostles Brigham Young, Heber Kimball, and Willard Richards, as well as a few trusted others into the sacred space. He spent the day giving them a ritual washing, a symbolic anointing, and lessons of light and knowledge. He taught what they needed to know to regain God's presence and abide there. These were "things spiritual," Joseph said, "and to be received only by the spiritual minded."[3]

Joseph intended to give the endowment of power to everyone who wanted it.[4] He promised to give it to the sisters. He told them they would see "the blessings of the endowment rolling on."[5] He began to give it to the sisters on September 28, 1843. That day, in their home across the street from his store, Joseph officiated as God endowed Emma with power.[6] Joseph and Emma then gave the ordinances to others. Preparing for the next endowment meeting, Emma met in her bedroom with a few Relief Society sisters and gave them the symbolic washing and anointing. A week later, she did the same for her mother-in-law Lucy, her counselor Elizabeth Ann Whitney, and a few others. Emma continued to wash and anoint sisters that fall. Joseph, meanwhile, taught the Saints in October conference to "hasten the work of the temple."[7]

On March 24, 1844, Joseph preached at the temple again, though not the doctrinally rich discourse the Saints were getting used to hearing. Instead he shared the shocking news that his former counselor William Law and other enemies inside Nauvoo were conspiring to kill him.[8] On March 26, 1844, rain drizzled outside as the endowed apostles and many of Nauvoo's high priests met in the room above Joseph's store. He was as gloomy as the sky. "Brethren," he said, "the Lord bids me hasten the work in which we are engaged. He will not suffer that you should wait for your endowment until the temple is done. Some important scene is near to take place. It may be that my enemies will kill me, and in case they should, and the keys and power which rest upon me not be imparted to you, they will be lost from the Earth; but if I can only succeed in placing them upon your heads, then let me fall victim to murderous hands if God will suffer it, and I can go with all pleasure and satisfaction, knowing that my work is done, and the foundation is laid on which the kingdom of God is to be reared in this dispensation of the fulness of times."[9]

The nine apostles in the room had received all of the temple ordinances. They held the keys that Joseph had received from angels.

They were the ones who could carry the work forward without Joseph. "Upon the shoulders of the Twelve must the responsibility of leading this church hence forth rest until you shall appoint others to succeed you," Joseph told them. He was candid about what was at stake. "Should any of you be killed, you can lay your hands upon others and fill up your quorum. Thus can this power and these keys be perpetuated in the earth." Joseph's face brightened as his burden began to lighten. "I roll the burthen and responsibility of leading this church off my shoulders and onto yours," he said as he finished, "the Lord is going to let me rest a while."[10]

Three months later, Joseph was murdered at Carthage, Illinois. But he had specifically commissioned Brigham Young to succeed him as the one man on earth at a time who exercises the key of the priesthood mentioned in Doctrine and Covenants 132:7. "This last key of the priesthood is the most sacred of all, and pertains exclusively to the first presidency of the church, without whose sanction and approval or authority, no sealing blessing shall be administered pertaining to things of the resurrection and the life to come."[11] Joseph Smith also gave Brigham Young the responsibility of organizing the temple ordinances. Brigham remembered how Joseph endowed him and gave him the job of carrying on. He said:

> Joseph divided up the room the best that he could hung up the veil, marked it gave us our instructions as we passed along from one department to another giving us signs, tokens, penalties with the Key words pertaining to those signs and after we had got through. Bro Joseph turned to me (Pres B. Young) and said Bro Brigham this is not arranged right but we have done the best we could under the circumstances in

which we are placed, and I. . . . wish you to take this matter in hand and organize and systematize all these ceremonies with the signs, tokens penalties and Key words I did so and each time I got something more so that when we went through the Temple at Nauvoo I understood and Knew how to place them there, we had our ceremonies pretty correct.[12]

Of all the would-be successors to Joseph Smith, only Brigham Young, the president of the Quorum of Twelve Apostles, understood what was at stake. He explained what was at stake to the Saints on August 8, 1844. Many, including Martha Tuttle Gardner, received their own revelations that Brigham Young was the Lord's choice to lead them. She testified that Brigham Young "told the people that although Joseph was dead, Joseph had left behind the keys of the Kingdom and had conferred the same power & authority that he himself possessed upon the Twelve Apostles and the Church would not be left without a leader and a guide."[13] "Don't scatter," Brigham told the Saints who gathered at the grove to hear him as they had Joseph. "Stay here in Nauvoo," he taught them, "build up the Temple and get your endowment."[14]

Before the Saints could finish the temple and receive the endowment, legislators revoked Nauvoo's charter, undoing their earlier law that promised citizens their own schools, courts, and especially their own militia unit to protect them. That sent Brigham to his knees, where he asked the Lord if the Saints should still stay and finish the temple. Yes, came the simple reply. So they did. Brigham taught the Saints the law of consecration. He pled with them to offer all they had, urging them not to think of their property as *theirs*, "but all things are the Lord's and we are his stewards." Brigham called most of the missionaries home to help finish the temple. He visited the site often to encourage and praise the workers.[15]

In May 1845, the apostles laid the capstone.[16] Even as they gave their all to finish the House of the Lord, the Saints sensed that their worship within its walls would be short-lived. The temple, they knew, was a means to the end. That end was eternal life. In the meantime, they would need another place to gather and build another temple, and they planned to seek this one far away, in the West. By October, the temple's interior was finished enough for the Saints to fill it up for general conference. Brigham proposed that once they were endowed, they would all move west together, leaving none behind, no matter how poor. The Saints raised their hands as a testimony that they would follow him. "If you will be faithful to your covenant," he told them, "I will now prophesy that the great God will shower down means upon this people, to accomplish it."[17]

By mid-October 1845, as the Saints' enemies threatened to pull the roofs off every house in Nauvoo, the Saints pled with God to protect them so they could finish the temple and be endowed with His power. By late November, the temple workers had plastered walls, carpeted floors, and hung curtains in the highest rooms. The leaders of the Church met there, dedicated the rooms, and reviewed the ordinances. Then, with a flock of workers—women and men to wash, anoint, and endow them—the anxious Saints were admitted into the temple and the work began. Night and day they came. Brigham supervised, repeating the ordinances hundreds of times, sleeping a few hours here and there, going home just once a week.[18]

When the Saints were not making the covenant to consecrate, they were acting on it. When Brigham was not endowing the Saints, he was organizing them into companies committed to caring for each other on the way west. Brigham pushed the leaders of each company to prepare their people and report. How many were ready and willing to start at a moment's notice? He knew by now that they would leave Nauvoo before the prairie grass grew high enough to feed their animals or the ice had thawed on the streams. But it was that or be murdered, as Brother Durfee was, or have their homes burned, as the Morleys had. So they prayed for time, and planned to be off just as soon as they were endowed. "One hundred and twenty-eight persons received ordinances in the Temple. I continued ministering at the altar," Brigham noted one day. The next day "one hundred and fifty persons received ordinances in the Temple." The next week he learned that the governor wanted to keep the saints from leaving. Brigham endowed Saints until ten that evening and spent the night in the House of the Lord.

The next day he and others worked late again, endowing one hundred seventy-two souls. And so it continued, day after day, as "one hundred and thirty-three persons received ordinances" and "one hundred and seventy-two persons received the ordinances of endowment." Brigham and the small army of sisters and brothers carefully ministered to every single Latter-day Saint who was prepared and willing to make the covenants, including consecration. On January 31, "two hundred and thirty-three persons received ordinances," Brigham noted. The next day he called for a council of the Saints to make final plans for departure. It was time to go. The next day "two hundred and thirty-four persons received ordinances," and Brigham sent messengers to the captains, telling them everyone should be ready to leave within four hours. Then Brigham continued endowing the Saints until late into the night.[19]

When Brigham arose the next day, Saints were crowding the

temple, anxious for their turn to be endowed. It was not wise, Brigham told them. If they stayed any longer, their way west could be cut off. He assured them there would be more temples, more opportunities to be endowed, and that all their efforts in Nauvoo's temple were worthwhile even if they got no more. But the Saints still craved the sacred ordinances and covenants for which they had consecrated so much. Brigham walked away, saying he was going to get his wagon and leave, thinking that would signal how serious he was about not giving any more ordinances until the Saints were safely somewhere in the West. But no one else moved. They were serious too. Finally, Brigham turned, retraced his steps, walked up into the temple, and went back to work until two hundred and ninety-five more Saints were endowed with power.[20]

Martha Tuttle Gardner wrote of witnessing the Prophet Joseph Smith and she knew she could transfer the title of Prophet to Brigham Young. She wrote that he "had the Nauvoo Temple finished" and endowed her with power there early in 1845. Then Martha and many other consecrated Saints fled Nauvoo for peace and safety somewhere they could keep their covenants.[21]

21.

Continuity, Change, and the Ongoing Restoration

In 1846, Brigham Young led the Saints across Iowa Territory, and they camped for the winter on the banks of the Missouri River. There, in a January 1847 council meeting, the Prophet Brigham Young asked the Lord to reveal "the best manner of organizing companies for emigration." The Lord answered.[1]

Key words in the revelation are *organized* and *covenant*. The Saints were to be organized into companies. "And this shall be our covenant—that we will walk in all the ordinances of the Lord" (Doctrine and Covenants 136:4). Like Martha Tuttle Gardner, many of them had recently made temple covenants in Nauvoo. The revelation declares the consequence of failing to keep the covenants they had made: "And if any man shall seek to build himself up, and seeketh not my counsel, he shall have no *power*, and his folly shall be made manifest" (Doctrine and Covenants 136:19; emphasis added). So the endowment of *power* is dependent on keeping the covenants made in the endowment ordinance.

By 1846, there are records of adults being sealed to adults who were not previously members of the same family—what became known as the law of adoption. Many Saints at this time were adult converts whose choice to join and gather with other Saints wrenched them from their families. At the time, no one was sealed to deceased ancestors that were not known to have already accepted the gospel while living. The Saints assumed that they should be sealed to other Saints, and especially those who were likely to be exalted. So the apostles developed large families of adopted adult children and their families. The migration from Nauvoo to the West was organized in part by these families. Given the fallen nature of people, jealousies developed between families, as well as a hierarchy of superior and inferior families.

In Winter Quarters, camped on the Missouri River en route to the West in February 1846, Brigham Young was sick and worried about the law of adoption. He knew sealing was key to exaltation but confessed that "I have had only a smattering [of knowledge] of those things but when it is necessary I will attain to more knowledge of the subject & consequently will be enabled to teach."[2] Soon after that, Brigham Young dreamed that he went to see Joseph Smith. During their conversation, Brigham said, "The Brethren have grate anxiety to understand the law of adoption or sealing principles," and asked for counsel. Joseph replied, "Tell the people to be humble and faithful and sure to keep the Spirit of the Lord and it will lead them right. . . . Tell the brethren [to] keep their harts open . . . so that when the Holy Gost comes to them there harts will be ready to receive it. They can tell the Spirit of the Lord from all other Spirits. It will whisper peace and joy to their soles and it will take malice, hatred, envying, strife, and all evil from their harts, and their whole desire will be to do good, bring forth righteousness, and build up the Kingdom of God. Tell the Brethren if they will follow the Spirit of the Lord they will go right.'"[3]

One Sunday a few months later, shortly after they arrived in the Salt Lake Valley, Brigham Young and other apostles spoke about the ordinances given in Nauvoo, what they planned to do now that they were in the West, and how adoption figured into their plans. Wilford Woodruff recorded their teachings. Endowment ordinances resumed in Utah Territory in 1852; they were performed in a special "Endowment House" on Temple Square by the mid-1850s. President Young sent Wilford Woodruff to preside over the St. George temple when it opened in 1877, with explicit plans to begin the work of endowments for the dead. Up to this point, the endowment ordinances had been transmitted orally, with considerable variation. President Young tasked St. George temple president and apostle Wilford Woodruff, along with a committee of recorders, to "write out the Ceremony of the Endowments from Beginning to End."[4]

Ever since it was first restored, the endowment has been characterized by both change and continuity. It is still a pageant about God's purposeful plan for His children that focuses on creation, fall, and redemption through Jesus Christ. A core set of covenants and promises has remained consistent. So has the sacred garment associated with the endowment. But the patterns and fabric of the garment have changed many times. So have many other things related to the endowment. Some things have been added, some subtracted, and the way it is presented has changed often.

Given this history of continuity and change, the endowment of power must not be in the things that change. It is in the things that stay the same: 1) the core doctrine of the plan of redemption, 2) our covenants to obey God's laws, and 3) the promised blessings of redemption through Christ's Atonement that empower us to regain God's presence.

When President John Taylor presided over the Lord's Church, he wished—like Brigham Young had earlier—that Joseph had revealed more. Acknowledging that there was still restoration work to be done with temple ordinances, President Taylor explained, "Joseph felt called upon to confer all ordinances connected with the Priesthood. He felt in a hurry on account of [a] certain premonition that he had concerning his death, and was very desirous to impart the endowments and all the ordinances thereof to the Priesthood during his lifetime." President Taylor felt that if Joseph had lived longer "he would have had much more to say on many of those points which he was prevented from doing by his death." Because he discerned that "great carelessness and a lack of appreciation had been manifested by many who had partaken of these sacred ordinances," President Taylor slowed down the process by which the Saints received all the ordinances of exaltation, giving them time to prove the faithfulness on which all their covenant blessings depended.[5]

Like Brigham Young and John Taylor, all of the prophets who followed Joseph sought and received more revelation to help them solve the challenges and problems associated with their commission to give the Saints temple covenants and ordinances. As he contemplated the challenges he faced, President Wilford Woodruff remembered that, in Nauvoo, Joseph taught the Saints to "redeem our dead and connect ourselves with our fathers which are in heaven and seal up our dead to come forth in the first resurrection. . . . Go and seal on earth your sons and daughters unto yourself and yourself unto your fathers [and mothers] in eternal glory." President Woodruff realized:

> We have not fully carried out those principles in fulfillment of the revelations of God to us, in sealing the hearts of the fathers to the children and the children to the fathers. I have not felt satisfied, neither did President [John] Taylor, neither has any man since the Prophet Joseph who has attended to the ordinance of adoption in the temples of our God. We have felt that there was more to be revealed upon this subject than we had received.[6]

Some of that additional revelation came to President Woodruff on April 5, 1894. Three days later, in a general conference address, he told of the revelation, saying that he and the prophets before him felt "that we have got to have more revelation concerning sealing." He told about a personal revelation he had received earlier when he sought to know who he should be sealed to.

> The Spirit of God said to me, 'Have you not a father, who begot you?' 'Yes, I have.' 'Then why not honor him? Why not be adopted to him?' 'Yes,' says I, 'that is right.' I was adopted to my father, and should have had my father sealed to his father, and so on back; and the duty that I want every man who presides over a temple to see performed from this day henceforth and forever, unless the Lord Almighty commands otherwise, is, let every man be adopted to his father. When a man receives the endowments, adopt him to his father; not to Wilford Woodruff, nor to any other man outside the lineage of his fathers. That is the will of God to this people.[7]

This, President Woodruff said, fulfilled

exactly what God said when he declared he would send Elijah the prophet in the last days. Elijah the prophet appeared unto Joseph Smith and told him that the day had come when this principle must be carried out. Joseph Smith did not live long enough to enter any further upon these things. His soul was wound up with this work before he was martyred for the word of God and testimony of Jesus Christ. He told us that there must be a welding link of all dispensations and of the work of God from one generation to another. This was upon his mind more than most any other subject that was given to him.[8]

Ever since the Lord's April 1894 revelation to Wilford Woodruff, Latter-day Saints have done sealings genealogically to ancestors rather than by being adopted into other families. And the prophets have admonished the saints, as Joseph Smith did, to present the records of ancestors in the temples for ordinances (see Doctrine and Covenants 128).

In that same landmark conference talk in which Wilford Woodruff announced the Lord's latest revelation to him, he taught us to expect more. "I want to say, as the President of the Church of Jesus Christ of Latter-day Saints, that we should now go on and progress. We have not got through revelation. We have not got through the work of God." He added, "We have had prophets and apostles. President Young who followed President Joseph Smith, led us here. He organized these Temples and carried out the purposes of his calling and office. . . . He accomplished all that God required at his hands. But he did not receive all the revelations that belong to this work; neither did President Taylor, nor has Wilford Woodruff. There will be no end to this work until it is perfected."[9]

Wilford Woodruff lived long enough to bear his testimony into Thomas Edison's phonograph, recording his voice on wax cylinders that are preserved in the Church History Library in Salt Lake City. He emphasized continuity.[10] He got his temple ordinances and his apostolic commission under Joseph's direction. Those same ordinances and the commission to give them to the Saints is now vested in the Lord's living prophet and apostles. They continue the work of Elijah the prophet announced by Moroni on September 21, 1823, which Joseph pushed forward unto death, handed off to Brigham Young, and so on.

The Lord's living prophets and apostles have the Lord's power (priesthood) and commission (keys) to continue this work, including overseeing continuity and change as needed. If their temple emphasis is any indication, they are wholeheartedly committed to resolving the remaining priesthood problems of endowing and sealing every one of God's children who wants to make and keep covenants. In 2021, President Russell M. Nelson showed the Saints how "we are performing major renovations on the historic Salt Lake Temple."[11] He told us the story of continuity and change this chapter tells, summing it up with the statement of these three truths:

1. The Restoration is a process, not an event, and will continue until the Lord comes again.
2. The ultimate objective of the gathering of Israel is to bring the blessings of the temple to God's faithful children.
3. As we seek how to accomplish *that* objective more

effectively, the Lord reveals more insights. The ongoing Restoration needs ongoing revelation.[12]

The work of preserving and renewing the Salt Lake Temple is like the continuity and change that characterizes temple ordinances over time. In 2019 the First Presidency announced, "With the restoration of the gospel in these latter days, temple worship has also been restored to bless the lives of people across the world and on the other side of the veil as well. Over these many centuries, details associated with temple work have been adjusted periodically, including language, methods of construction, communication, and record-keeping. Prophets have taught that there will be no end to such adjustments as directed by the Lord to His servants."[13]

If we think too fast, we might assume that any change in temple-related teachings and ordinances is wrong. But we can identify and interrogate that assumption and discover that it is unfounded. The Lord has not said it. His prophets have not taught it. Rather, the Lord's precedent and practice has been to restore temple-related teachings, covenants, and ordinances as an ongoing process. Joseph taught that to the Saints in an 1842 letter:

> It is necessary in the ushering in of the dispensation of the fulness of times, which dispensation is now beginning to usher in, that a whole and complete and perfect union, and welding together of dispensations, and keys, and powers, and glories should take place, and be revealed from the days of Adam even to the present time. And not only this, but those things which never have been revealed from the foundation of the world, but have been kept hid from the wise and prudent, shall be revealed unto babes and sucklings in

this, the dispensation of the fulness of times. (Doctrine and Covenants 128:18)

Then Joseph started listing events he had experienced in the ongoing process of restoration, events in which ministering angels gave him "their dispensation, their rights, their keys, their honors, their majesty and glory, and the power of their priesthood; giving line upon line; precept upon precept; here a little, and there a little" (Doctrine and Covenants 128:21). He asked, "Shall we not go on in so great a cause," meaning God's plan "before the world was" to redeem and seal every person in the human family who desires the blessings Christ promises to everyone who makes and keeps covenants (Doctrine and Covenants 128:22).

That is the cause of Christ. It is the work of His restored Church. We choose whether or not to be part of it.

22.

All Are Alike unto God

In March 1830, the first calfskin-bound copies of the Book of Mormon were advertised for sale by Egbert Grandin's print shop in Palmyra, New York. If we had walked into the shop that day, picked up a copy, and turned to pages 108 and 109, we could have read the words of the mature Nephi: the old man, looking back on a lifetime of lessons learned, of reading and internalizing Isaiah's teachings. Nephi had come to understand, as he wrote: "Hath the Lord commanded any that they should not partake of his goodness? Behold I say unto you, Nay; . . . none are forbidden. . . . He inviteth them all to come unto him, and partake of his goodness; and he denieth none that come unto him, black and white, bond and free, male and female; and he remembereth the heathen; and all are alike unto God, both Jew and Gentile" (2 Nephi 26:28, 33).

That was the doctrine of The Church of Jesus Christ when it was organized a week later, on April 6, 1830, so in this chapter I will call it the *day one doctrine*, meaning that it was the revealed doctrine of the Savior's church from the day it was restored. Nephi's teaching in 2 Nephi 26:33 has always been the Church's doctrine. It is today. President Nelson has cited and taught it repeatedly. But between 1847 and 1852, the Church implemented a racial restriction. From then until 1978, Black Saints were not given the temple endowment or sealing ordinances, and Black men were not ordained to priesthood offices.

Oliver Cowdery, Parley Pratt, and other missionaries took copies of the Book of Mormon to Ohio, and at least one of their converts was a person of color, a man we only know as Peter or Pete. He was born at the beginning of the American Revolution in Western Pennsylvania to an enslaved woman named Kino. Peter was one of six free Black people in Geauga County, Ohio, in 1820. He worshiped with the Saints, who were unpopular with their neighbors and in the country at large, so Peter's presence among the Saints was put forth as evidence that they were guilty of miscegenation (racial mixing or intermarriage—considered a heinous offense by nearly all white people at the time, including most Saints). We know precious little about Peter—we do not know if he died or chose not to stick with the Saints. We do not know if the Saints chose not to stick with him. There is no known record of his baptism, and nothing is known of him after 1831.[1]

By the time the Church was organized in 1830, Africans and their descendants had been enslaved in the Americas for over two centuries. Seeking to justify their enslavement of Africans, Europeans searched for and found rationalizations by combining the Bible and unsound assumptions. Genesis 9 reports that Noah cursed his grandson Canaan to be a servant. Though the passage says nothing about race, some whites cited it as justification for enslaving Africans.

Other scriptures were used to justify race-based slavery. Anti-slavery advocates used the Bible too, and the Bible itself became a battleground in the conflict for white superiority over Black people.[2]

The Church emerged in the midst of this ongoing controversy. Nothing was more frequently in the news or engaged the passions of Joseph Smith's fellow Americans more than the race-based antagonisms that led finally to Civil War, as Joseph prophesied (see Doctrine and Covenants 87). Early Latter-day Saints had varied opinions, assumptions, prejudices—including slave ownership by some Saints, despite the Lord's revelation to Joseph that "it is not right that any man should be in bondage one to another" because all people are divinely endowed with "moral agency" to act for themselves (Doctrine and Covenants 101:77–79). Then, as now, the Saints were not immune to what President Russell M. Nelson called "attitudes and actions of prejudice."[3] Then, as now, Saints did not always align with the Book of Mormon teaching that Jesus Christ invites all to come unto Him, denying none who do, whether they are black or white, male or female, Jew or Gentile (see 2 Nephi 26:33).

Compared to Peter, we know quite a bit about Elijah Abel. He was born in Maryland in 1810, maybe into slavery. He encountered the restored gospel in Cincinnati, was baptized at age twenty-two in 1832, and remained faithful to his covenants for the rest of his life. He was ordained an elder on January 25, 1836. On March 31, 1836, Joseph Smith signed a certificate stating that Elijah had been "ordained an Elder" and authorized to preach the gospel and was of high moral character and in full fellowship with the Saints.[4] Elijah was ordained by Zebedee Coltrin, a president of the Seventy, as a member of the Third Quorum of Seventy on December 20, 1836. He received his patriarchal blessing from Joseph Smith Sr. It noted that he had been "ordained an elder." He received washing and anointing ordinances in the house of the Lord at Kirtland. He faithfully served multiple missions. He was baptized for the dead in Nauvoo.[5]

Between the time Peter began worshipping with the Saints and Elijah got baptized, the Lord "appointed and consecrated" Missouri "for the gathering of the saints" (Doctrine and Covenants 57:1). Geographically, it was "the land of promise, and the place for the city of Zion," but culturally speaking, it was a long, long way from the holy city the scriptures prophesied (Doctrine and Covenants 57:2; see also Revelation 3:12; 21:2; 3 Nephi 20:22; 21:23–24; and Ether 13:3–6, 10). Early in the summer of 1831, the first time the Lord specified the place to Joseph Smith, He called it "the land of Missouri, which is the land of your inheritance, which is now the land of your enemies" (Doctrine and Covenants 52:42). Why were Missourians in the 1830s enemies of Zion?

The 1820 compromise that created Missouri as a slave state also surrounded it with free soil on three sides. Jackson County lay along Missouri's far western edge and south of the Missouri River, on the western border of the United States, where only an imaginary line separated the settlers from Indian Territory. Those Missouri settlers believed they were citizens who justifiably could subject other people. They depended on dispossessed Native Americans for the economic lifeblood that sustained Independence, Missouri. And they depended on the people they enslaved. One analyst showed that "Jackson County slave owners held tenaciously to their bondsmen because slavery was a thriving and profitable institution in that area of Missouri."[6] Jackson County's 2,600 settlers owned 193 human beings in 1830. At the same time the Saints were gathering to

Jackson County, the other white settlers there were tripling in number and those settlers were enslaving Black people at a much higher rate than that.

A British tourist of North America noted what he learned from a person who was well acquainted with the Saints. He said they "maintain the natural equality of mankind, without excepting the native Indians or the African race, [so] there is little reason to be surprised at the cruel persecution by which they have suffered." He concluded that "believers of the following doctrines were not likely to remain, unmolested, in Missouri," then cited 2 Nephi 26:33 specifically, saying the Lord invites "all to come unto him and partake of his goodness; and he denieth none that come unto him, black and white, bond and free, male and female; and he remembereth the heathen; and all are alike unto God, both Jew and Gentile."[7] So when hundreds of Latter-day Saint immigrants to Jackson County, Missouri, soon grew to a few thousand, the earlier white settlers worried that the mostly northern Saints would encourage the people they enslaved to seek freedom.

That is what white Jackson County residents thought William Phelps was doing when he published an article in the Church's newspaper in July 1833 titled "Free People of Color," and another article in the same issue in which he celebrated the growth of abolitionist sentiments in the country.[8] Those acts incited the neighbors to draft a "secret constitution" that accused the Saints of nurturing slave revolts and encouraging free Blacks to join them in the area. William Phelps backtracked and published an "Extra" in which he said that his actual intent had been to "not only stop free people of color from emigrating to this state but to prevent them from being admitted as members of the Church."[9] That is not what the Book of Mormon said. But it was the first of many times that, when push came to shove, white Saints sold out Black Saints and sided with majority sentiments instead of the day one doctrine of 2 Nephi 26:33.

In 1847, Brigham Young praised a Black priesthood holder named Q. Walker Lewis as "one of the best elders."[10] Then in 1850, the United States made another compromise that created Utah Territory. According to the Church's essay "Race and the Priesthood," Brigham Young declared to the territorial legislature in 1852 that Black men would no longer be ordained to the priesthood, at least not for the time being. A record of President Young's remarks says:

> The Lord told Cain [that] he should not receive the priesthood nor his seed, until the last of the posterity of Able had received the priesthood, until the redemption of the earth. If there never was a prophet, or apostle of Jesus Christ spoke it before, I tell you, this people that are commonly called negroes are the children of old Cain. I know they are, I know they cannot bear rule in the priesthood, for the curse on them, until the resedue of the posterity of Michael and his wife receive the blessings, the seed of Cain would have received had they not been cursed.[11]

President Young also said, "That time will come when they [Black people] will have the privilege of all we have and more." Brigham Young shared his culture's objection to interracial marriage. He said it would bring the curse of Cain upon white people. The Church's 2013 essay "Race and the Priesthood" describes this idea. It says:

> The justifications for this restriction echoed the widespread ideas about racial inferiority that had been used to

argue for the legalization of black 'servitude' in the Territory of Utah. According to one view, which had been promulgated in the United States from at least the 1730s, blacks descended from the same lineage as the biblical Cain, who slew his brother Abel. Those who accepted this view believed that God's 'curse' on Cain was the mark of a dark skin.[12]

That is not the day one doctrine of 2 Nephi 26:33. Nor is it the Church's doctrine today.[13] In fact, "Race and the Priesthood" explicitly disavows ideas that were (and to some extent still are) held by many Latter-day Saints:

> Today, the Church disavows the theories advanced in the past that black skin is a sign of divine disfavor or curse . . . that mixed-race marriages are a sin; or that blacks or people of any other race or ethnicity are inferior in any way to anyone else. Church leaders today unequivocally condemn all racism, past and present, in any form.[14]

Speaking generically about "a statement made by a Church leader decades ago that seems incongruent with our doctrine," Elder Neil L. Andersen taught, "There is an important principle that governs the doctrine of the Church. The doctrine is taught by all 15 members of the First Presidency and Quorum of the Twelve. It is not hidden in an obscure paragraph of one talk. True principles are taught frequently and by many. Our doctrine is not difficult to find."[15] By that standard, it is not necessarily doctrine that the Lord will always prevent a prophet from erring. That teaching is not in the scriptures, even though President Woodruff said in an 1890 general conference, "The Lord will never permit me or any other man who stands as President of this Church to lead you astray."[16] In 2007, the Church issued this statement:

> Not every statement made by a Church leader, past or present, necessarily constitutes doctrine. A single statement made by a single leader on a single occasion often represents a personal, though well-considered, opinion, but is not meant to be officially binding for the whole Church. With divine inspiration, the First Presidency (the prophet and his two counselors) and the Quorum of the Twelve Apostles (the second-highest governing body of the Church) counsel together to establish doctrine that is consistently proclaimed in official Church publications. This doctrine resides in the four "standard works" of scripture (the Holy Bible, the Book of Mormon, the Doctrine and Covenants and the Pearl of Great Price), official declarations and proclamations, and the Articles of Faith. Isolated statements are often taken out of context, leaving their original meaning distorted.[17]

It is not exactly clear what President Woodruff meant by the isolated statement quoted above. What is clear is that various apostles have repeatedly acknowledged that "the leaders of the Church are honest but imperfect men" and "there have been times when members or leaders in the Church have simply made mistakes. There may have been things said or done that were not in harmony with our values, principles, or doctrine."[18] The apostles remind us that neither the Lord nor His servants have claimed that the Lord's mortal servants are error-free. Rather, they point us to the Savior—whose servants they (and we) are—as our infallible guide.

Nearly two years after Brigham Young's death in 1877, Elijah

Abel asked to receive his temple ordinances. That prompted John Taylor to investigate the origins of the race-based restrictions. Zebedee Coltrin told President Taylor that he and John Greene had argued in 1834 about whether Black men could hold the priesthood. Greene said they could. Coltrin said they could not, and they decided to ask Joseph when they next saw him. According to Coltrin, Joseph said "Brother Zebedee is right, for the spirit of the Lord saith the Negro has not right nor cannot hold the priesthood," but Zebedee's memory needs to be weighed in the balance of all the sources of our knowledge about Elijah's ordination. Joseph signed Elijah Abel's ministering license in March 1836 and Zebedee himself ordained Elijah a Seventy in December 1836. Zebedee said that Joseph dropped Elijah from the quorum when he learned of his lineage. Apostle Joseph F. Smith questioned Zebedee's memory and concluded that Joseph Smith always recognized Elijah's ordination. John Taylor decided to let Elijah's ordination stand but prohibited him from receiving temple ordinances. A few years later, Elijah served a third mission, then died shortly thereafter, firm in the faith he had embraced in his early twenties.

Another Black Latter-day Saint, Jane Elizabeth Manning James, entered the restored covenant by baptism in 1841. Her autobiography says:

> When about fourteen years old, I joined the Presbyterian Church. Yet I did not feel satisfied; it seemed to me there was something more that I was looking for. I had belonged to the Church about eighteen months when an elder of The Church of Jesus Christ of Latter-day Saints was traveling through our country [and] preached there. The pastor of the Presbyterian

Church forbid me going to hear them—as he had heard I had expressed a desire to hear them—but nevertheless, I went on a Sunday and was fully convinced that it was the true gospel he presented and I must embrace it. The following Sunday I was baptized and confirmed a member of The Church of Jesus Christ of Latter-day Saints.[19]

About a year later, Jane led her mother, siblings, and other relatives to Nauvoo, walking most of the way after they were denied boat passage at Buffalo because they were Black. Joseph and Emma Smith welcomed Jane and her family into their home, listened to their story, and helped them find housing and employment. Jane lived with and worked for Emma and Joseph, who invited her to be sealed to them as a daughter. Jane declined, explaining, "I did not understand or know what it meant. They were always good and kind to me, but I did not know my own mind. I did not comprehend." Joseph was murdered. Jane was never sealed to anyone. She crossed the plains and pioneered with her fellow Saints.

In 1884, Jane wrote to President John Taylor. She knew the terms of God's covenant with Abraham, which had recently been canonized in the Pearl of Great Price:

I will make of thee a great nation, and I will bless thee above measure, and make thy name great among all nations, and thou shalt be a blessing unto thy seed after thee, that in their hands they shall bear this ministry and Priesthood unto all nations; And I will bless them through thy name; for as many as receive this Gospel shall be called after thy name, and shall be accounted thy seed, and shall rise up and bless thee, as their father; . . . for I give unto thee a promise that

this right shall continue in thee, and in thy seed after thee . . .
shall all the families of the earth be blessed, even with the
blessings of the Gospel, which are the blessings of salvation,
even of life eternal. (Abraham 2:9–11)

Jane told President Taylor that she was the only member of her
family who remained faithful to the covenant. She explained the
invitation Joseph and Emma offered her. She told President Taylor,
"If I could be adopted to him [Joseph] as a child, my soul would be
satisfied." She noted that God had covenanted with Abraham that
his posterity would bless all nations. "As this is the fulness of all dispensations," Jane asked, "is there no blessing for me?" She closed her
letter with a prayer, asking God to grant her request, and signed it,
"I remain your Sister in the gospel of Christ."[20] Jane was allowed to
be baptized for her deceased loved ones.[21]

Years later, Jane was worried about what would become of
her when she died. Even if she lived to see the Salt Lake temple
completed, she was not sure she could receive the ordinances to be
offered in it. Her husband had left her. Four of her children had
passed away, along with several of her grandchildren. She had not
been sealed to them, and she worried whether they would belong to
each other when she died. Would she belong with anyone?

She could take comfort from her recent patriarchal blessing. It
said the Lord had heard her prayers, knew her heart, and promised that she would eventually be satisfied. But for now, Jane felt
unsatisfied about three things. She wrote about them to Joseph F.
Smith, counselor in the First Presidency: First, Jane said, her husband had left her twenty-one years earlier, but Q. Walker Lewis, one
of few Black men to be ordained to the priesthood, had wished to

be sealed to Jane before his death. "When, or can I ever, be sealed to him[?]" Jane asked. "I had the privilege of being baptized for my dead," she added, "can I obtain endowments for my dead also[?]" Finally, Jane explained, "Emma said Joseph told her to tell me I could be adopted in their family. She ask[ed] me if I should like to. I did not understand the law of adoption then but understanding it now, can that be accomplished and when[?]"[22]

Jane waited for an answer from the First Presidency. She longed for an answer she never received. She keenly felt the tension between verifiable facts—the fact that she was forbidden to receive the fulness of the gospel covenant, and the fact, as Jane articulated it to President Taylor, that "God promised Abraham that in his seed all the nations of the earth should be blest [so] . . . is there no blessing for me." Jane waited faithfully for fulness in that tension, even when Church leaders allowed her to be "attached" to Emma and Joseph Smith as a servant rather than sealed to them as a daughter. It wasn't the promise she'd been waiting for, so she continued to ask for her full, promised temple blessings. Even without receiving them, she remained ever and always a sister in the gospel of Jesus Christ.[23]

Before she died in 1908, Jane dictated her memoir. She told her story. She told how she chose to follow the prophets she could have rejected:

> I have seen Brother Brigham, Brothers Taylor, Woodruff, and Snow rule this great work and pass on to their reward, and now Brother Joseph F. Smith. I hope the Lord will spare him . . . for many, many years to guide the gospel ship to a harbor of safety, and I know they will, if the people will only listen and obey the teachings of these good, great, and holy

men. I have lived right here in Salt Lake City for fifty-two years, and I have had the privilege of going into the temple and being baptized for some of my dead. I am now over eighty years old, and I am nearly blind, which is a great trial to me. . . . But the Lord protects me and takes good care of me in my helpless condition, and I want to say right here that my faith in the gospel of Jesus Christ as taught by the Church of Jesus Christ of Latter-day Saints is as strong today, nay, it is, if possible, stronger than it was the day I was first baptized.[24]

When there is tension between verifiable facts of the Restoration, as there is in this case, we get to choose how to respond to them. In this case there is tension between the fact that the doctrine of the Savior's church has always been that Jesus Christ invites all to come to Him and denies none who choose Him, and the fact that by 1852, a race-based restriction prevented Black Latter-day Saints from receiving temple ordinances or holding priesthood offices. We could make any number of choices about how to respond to those two facts.

Jane Manning and Elijah Abel saw themselves included in the covenant and they clung to its promises with immense faith, undying hope, and true charity. Jane and Elijah intentionally chose faith, hope, and charity to cope with the unresolved tension. We can choose to have faith that the Lord calls prophets. We can choose charity for flawed brothers and sisters. We could choose to not condemn them, "but rather," as one imperfect prophet hoped, "give thanks unto God that he hath made manifest unto you our imperfections, that ye may learn to be more wise than we have been" (Mormon 9:31).

We can choose to have charity for past prophets while we follow our living prophets' counsel to root out racism and lead out in abandoning attitudes and actions of prejudice. President Russell M. Nelson has emphatically and repeated emphasized the day one doctrine that all are alike unto God. We get to choose. Jane Manning James and Elijah Abel can be our guides.

23.

The Long-Promised Day

This chapter tells how, in 1978, the Lord revealed the solution to the problem of a race-based temple and priesthood restriction that existed in the Church by 1852. It emphasizes how prophets have called on us to lead out in abandoning all remaining attitudes and actions of racial prejudice that remain with us and in us. We are to root them out for good.[1]

In 1908, the year Jane Manning James died, Joseph F. Smith was the President of the Savior's Church. That year, he said that Joseph Smith had nullified Elijah Abel's 1836 ordination to the priesthood. That was a reversal of John Taylor's 1879 decision that Elijah's ordination was an exception that was allowed to stand. That had been Joseph F. Smith's view at the time too, but by 1908 the First Presidency decided:

> The descendants of Ham may receive baptism and confirmation but no one known to have in his veins negro blood, (it matters not how remote a degree) can either have the

Priesthood in any degree or the blessings of the Temple of God; no matter how otherwise worthy he may be.[2]

By 1949, Church leaders assumed that it had always been that way:

> The attitude of the Church with reference to Negroes remains as it has always stood. It is not a matter of the declaration of policy but of direct commandment from the Lord.[3]

The tension between revealed gospel truths and the race-based restrictions compelled Latter-day Saints to reconcile the tension. Between 1852 and 1978, Latter-day Saints often tried to reconcile the two facts with interpretations based on folk doctrines—teachings that did not come from God, but from the Saints.

In 1907, Joseph Fielding Smith wrote a letter describing how these folk doctrines formed: "There is nothing in our standard works, nor any authoritative statement to the effect that one third of the hosts of heaven remained neutral in the great conflict and that the colored races are of that neutral class. The statement has been put forth at various times until the belief has become quite general that the Negro race has been cursed for taking a neutral position in that great contest. But this is not the official position of the Church merely the opinion of men."[4]

We can be confident in describing these teachings as folk doctrines for two reasons:

1. They sometimes contradict each other, and they contradict revealed doctrines like 2 Nephi 26:33; Doctrine and Covenants 36; 74; 93; and Article of Faith 2.
2. The Church has repudiated each of these teachings.[5]

The folk doctrines include the idea that Cain's descendants were cursed. The scriptures do not say that. The Book of Moses says that Cain's descendants were "black," but it does not say they inherited Cain's curse (Moses 7:22). President Young taught that "the posterity of Cane are Black Because He commit Murder He killed Abel & God set a Mark upon his posterity." Though there is no record of it in the scriptures, President Young also taught: "The Lord told Cain that he should not receive the blessings of the Priesthood, nor his seed, until the last of the posterity of Abel had received the priesthood."[6]

Historian W. Paul Reeve wrote, "Because the curse of Cain so directly violated the role of individual agency in the lives of Black people, some Latter-day Saints turned to the premortal realm to solve the conundrum. In this rationale, Black people must have been neutral in the War in Heaven and thus were cursed with black skin and barred from the priesthood."[7] Brigham Young rejected that reason, saying that he "herd Joseph say to the contrary all spirits are pure that come from the presence of God."[8] That truth is affirmed repeatedly in the scriptures (see Moroni 8; Doctrine and Covenants 74; 93). The folk doctrine of premortal neutrality persisted, however. It was used to reconcile the theological problem that resulted from the fact that the restriction existed in tension with the second article of faith and other scriptures that say that people are judged for the exercise of their agency, not their ancestors' exercise of agency.

The Bible says that both Cain (son of Adam and Eve) and Canaan (grandson of Noah) were cursed, but not that their posterity was cursed. Over time, these passages were interpreted to justify race-based slavery. By the 1800s, this interpretation was deeply ingrained among white Europeans and Americans.[9] Many Latter-day Saints persisted in believing and teaching that Black people descended from Cain and/or Canaan, and that they were cursed as a result.[10]

Elder Orson Pratt identified and interrogated those assumptions in 1856 in debates about whether Utah Territory should adopt slavery when he said, "We have no proof that Africans are the descendants of old Cain, who was cursed. And even if we had that evidence, we have not been ordered to inflict that [curse] upon that race."[11] That was highly unusual. Most Saints (and most white people generally) rarely identified or interrogated the assumptions they accepted about race and slavery. That is true for people who were righteous, smart, and knowledgeable.

For example, in a church magazine in 1885, General Authority B. H. Roberts assumed the validity of the curse of Cain idea, including the belief that all Black people descended from Cain and other people did not. He linked that idea with two scriptures from the Pearl of Great Price and added a variation on the premortal premise when he said, "Others there were [in premortality besides those who stood squarely with Satan], who may not have rebelled against God, and yet were so indifferent in their support of the righteous cause of our Redeemer, that they forfeited certain privileges and powers granted to those who were more valiant for God and correct principle."[12]

Elder Roberts drew from Abraham 1:25–26, which states, "Now the first government of Egypt was established by Pharaoh, the eldest son of Egyptus, the daughter of Ham, and it was after the manner of the government of Ham, which was patriarchal. Pharaoh, being a righteous man, established his kingdom and judged his people wisely and justly all his days, seeking earnestly to imitate that order established by the fathers in the first generations, in the days of the first patriarchal reign, even in the reign of Adam, and also of

Noah, his father, who blessed him with the blessings of the earth, and with the blessings of wisdom, but cursed him as pertaining to the Priesthood."

He then linked that with Moses 7:7–8, 22:

> And the Lord said unto me: Prophesy; and I prophesied, saying: Behold the people of Canaan, which are numerous, shall go forth in battle array against the people of Shum, and shall slay them that they shall utterly be destroyed; and the people of Canaan shall divide themselves in the land, and the land shall be barren and unfruitful, and none other people shall dwell there but the people of Canaan;
>
> For behold, the Lord shall curse the land with much heat, and the barrenness thereof shall go forth forever; and there was a blackness came upon all the children of Canaan, that they were despised among all people. . . .
>
> And Enoch also beheld the residue of the people which were the sons of Adam; and they were a mixture of all the seed of Adam save it was the seed of Cain, for the seed of Cain were black, and had not place among them.

B. H. Roberts had to make some unscriptural assumptions to arrive at his interpretation of the scriptures. Those assumptions included:

1. That Cain's curse included black skin. The Bible says Cain was cursed; Moses 7:22 says Cain's descendants were "black"; and neither says that Cain's curse included black skin. Now "the Church disavows the theories advanced in the past that black skin is a sign of divine disfavor or curse."[13]

2. That there was a genealogical link between Cain (the son of Eve and Adam, featured in Genesis 4) and Cannan (the grandson of Noah, featured in Genesis 9).

3. The meaning of the phrase, "cursed him as pertaining to the priesthood," which is not obvious or clear in scriptures (Abraham 1:26).

4. That Cain (who was cursed to be a fugitive and a vagabond in the earth and was marked with an unspecified mark, according to Moses 5:25–40), Pharaoh (who was "cursed as pertaining to priesthood," according to Abraham 1:26), and his brother-in-law Canaan (whom Noah cursed to be a servant, according to Genesis 9:22–27) all had shared posterity.

5. That Cain's curse, Pharoah's curse, and Canaan's curse were to be passed on to their descendants.

Elder Roberts wasn't the only one to make these kinds of assumptions. In 1907, Joseph Fielding Smith wrote that the premortal folk doctrine wasn't "the official position of the Church, merely the opinion of men." But in the 1960s, he adopted that opinion to explain that Black people were restricted because they "were not valiant" premortally.[14]

In 1958, a member of the Seventy named Bruce R. McConkie used both the curse of Cain and the premortal valiancy folk doctrines in his book *Mormon Doctrine.* In 1963, an apostle named Spencer W. Kimball expressed both frustration and faith regarding the race-based restriction. He said, "Admittedly our direct and positive information is limited. I have wished the Lord had given us a little more clarity on the matter." Elder Kimball did not know whether to characterize the restriction as a "doctrine or policy," but acknowledged that it "has not varied in my memory." He continued, "I know it could. I know the Lord could change his policy and release the ban and forgive the possible error which brought about the deprivation. If the time comes, that he will do, I am sure."[15]

In the context of this statement, it sounds like Elder Kimball was thinking that there were possible errors by Black people that led to them being restricted, but notice what that word *possible* does. It shows that Elder Kimball did not think he already knew everything about this issue. He thought slowly. He was open to possibilities and wanted more light and knowledge. One decade later, having survived repeated heart attacks and cancer in his throat, Spencer W. Kimball became the Lord's prophet. In April 1974, President Kimball gave the exhilarating talk, "When the World Will Be Converted":

> The scriptures are replete with commands and promises and calls and rewards for teaching the gospel. I use the word *command* deliberately, for it seems to be an insistent directive from which we, singly and collectively, cannot escape.
>
> I ask you, what did he mean when the Lord took his Twelve Apostles to the top of the Mount of Olives and said: "And ye shall be witnesses unto me both in Jerusalem, and in all Judea, and in Samaria, and unto the uttermost part of the earth" (Acts 1:8)?
>
> These were his last words on earth before he went to his heavenly home.
>
> What is the significance of the phrase "uttermost part of the earth"? He had already covered the area known to the apostles. Was it the people in Judea? Or those in Samaria? Or the few millions in the Near East? Where were the "uttermost

parts of the earth"? Did he mean the millions in what is now America? Did he include the hundreds of thousands, or even millions, in Greece, Italy, around the Mediterranean, the inhabitants of central Europe? What did he mean? Or did he mean all the living people of all the world and those spirits assigned to this world to come in centuries ahead? Have we underestimated his language or its meaning? . . .

After his crucifixion the eleven apostles assembled on a mountain in Galilee, and the Savior came to them and said: "All power is given unto me in heaven and in earth. Go ye therefore, and teach all nations, baptizing them in the name of the Father, and of the Son, and of the Holy Ghost."

(He said "all nations.")

"Teaching them to observe all things whatsoever I have commanded you: and, lo, I am with you alway, even unto the end of the world. Amen" (Matthew 28:18–20).[16]

Ramping up the Savior's great commission like that intensified the dissonance between the scriptures and the race-based restriction. President Kimball thought slowly and sought revelation to know how to fulfill the Savior's commission. He remembered:

I knew that something was before us that was extremely important to many of the children of God. I knew that we could receive the revelations of the Lord only by being worthy and ready for them and ready to accept them and put them into place. Day after day I went alone and with great solemnity and seriousness in the upper rooms of the temple, and there I offered my soul and offered my efforts to go forward with the program. I wanted to do what he wanted. I talked about it to him and said, "Lord, I want only what is right. We are not making any plans to be spectacularly moving. We want only the thing that thou dost want, and we want it when you want it and not until."[17]

President Kimball led the Lord's living apostles in a long, slow-thinking, revelatory process. Unknown to anyone except the First Presidency and the Apostles, President Kimball had asked each of them to carefully research the scriptures and statements of the earlier leaders, to make an exhaustive study of all that had been recorded concerning the restriction. For months before the June 1978 revelation, the First Presidency and Quorum of the Twelve discussed these things repeatedly in their temple meetings. President Kimball also met privately with each of the apostles to learn their thoughts and feelings on the matter.[18]

On Thursday, June 1, 1978, the general authorities held their regular monthly fast and testimony meeting. The members of the Seventy and the Presiding Bishopric were then excused, and President Kimball, his two counselors, and ten of the apostles remained (Elder Mark E. Peterson was on assignment in South America, and Elder Delbert L. Stapley was in the hospital). Before offering the prayer, President Kimball asked each of the brethren to express their views on this important issue. For more than two hours they talked freely and openly. Elder David B. Haight, the newest apostle at the time, observed, "As each responded, we witnessed an outpouring of the Spirit which bonded our souls together in perfect unity—a glorious experience. In that bond of unity we felt our total dependence upon heavenly direction if we were to more effectively accomplish the Lord's charge to carry the message of hope and salvation to *all* the world." Elder Haight continued, "President Kimball then suggested that we have our prayer at the altar. Usually he asked one of us to lead the prayer; however, on this day he asked, 'Would you mind if I be the voice at the altar today?'. . . . The prophet pleaded that he would be given the necessary direction which could expand the Church throughout the world by offering the fullness of the everlasting gospel to all men, based solely upon their personal worthiness without reference to race or color."[19]

President Kimball later said:

> We had the glorious experience of having the Lord indicate clearly that the time had come when all worthy men and women everywhere can be fellow heirs and partakers of the full blessings of the gospel. I want you to know, as a special witness of the Savior, how close I have felt to him and to our Heavenly Father as I have made numerous visits to the upper rooms in the temple, going on some days several times by myself. The Lord made it very clear to me what was to be done. We do not expect the people of the world to understand such things, for they will always be quick to assign their own reasons or to discount the divine process of revelation.[20]

One week after the revelation, on June 8, 1978, all available General Authorities met together in the Salt Lake Temple. They were told the Lord had affirmed by revelation that it was His will for them to remove the restrictions. They unanimously sustained that. President Kimball then put his hand on the knee of his counselor, N. Eldon Tanner, and said, "Go tell the world." Official Declaration 2 was released to the press a few minutes later. It is impossible to overstate how consequential that revelation was, and how joyfully it was received by so many Saints—black and white, male and female. But we can get a glimpse of it, a tiny taste, from "Be One—A Celebration of the Revelation on the Priesthood," a concert held on June 1, 2018, the fortieth anniversary of the revelation.[21]

So how can we make sense of this history? Speaking of 2 Nephi 26:33, Elder Bruce R. McConkie said, "These words have now taken on a new meaning. We have caught a new vision of their true significance. This also applies to a great number of other passages in the revelations. Since the Lord gave this revelation on the priesthood, our understanding of many passages has expanded. Many of us never imagined or supposed that they had the extensive and broad meaning that they do have."[22]

Elder McConkie acknowledged that he and others had misread 2 Nephi 26:33 and other scripture passages. "We spoke with a limited understanding," he said, "and without the light and knowledge that now has come into the world." To the assumption that prophets and apostles know everything, he taught, "We get our truth and our light line upon line and precept upon precept. We have now had added a new flood of intelligence and light on this particular subject, and it erases all the darkness and all the views and all the thoughts of the past." Elder McConkie invited anyone who wanted to go backward and not forward to accept and follow the Lord's latest revelation to His living prophet.[23]

W. Paul Reeve is the best historian of this part of our past. Rather than perpetuating the old ideas, he proposed an alternative interpretation of the verifiable facts:

> Perhaps it was and is a test that forces Latter-day Saints
> to search their hearts to see if they might summon the

courage and strength to rise above differences and embrace commonalities centered upon the worship of Jesus Christ. Could white Latter-day Saints transcend cultural norms and the privileges of being white in America, both before and after 1978, to welcome Black people into the gospel fold, into the priesthood, into the temple, and into their hearts? Could Black Latter-day Saints embrace a gospel message, both before and after 1978, that views them as children of God but that historically was burdened with teachings that they were cursed, less valiant, or neutral children of that same God?[24]

I choose to interpret this part of our past by listening to and learning from those who are understandably hurt by it.[25] One among many who inspires me is Jane Elizabeth Manning. I am strengthened by her choice to sustain prophets and apostles regardless of being restricted because of her race.

I choose to integrate President Jeffrey R. Holland's point into my slow-thinking process. He taught, "Except in the case of His only perfect Begotten Son, imperfect people are all God has ever had to work with. That must be terribly frustrating to Him, but He deals with it. So should we. And when you see imperfection, remember that the limitation is *not* in the divinity of the work. As one gifted writer has suggested, when the infinite fulness is poured forth, it is not the oil's fault if there is some loss because finite vessels can't quite contain it all. Those finite vessels include you and me, so be patient and kind and forgiving."[26]

In the same passage where he declared that Jesus Christ invites all to come to Him and denies none, black and white, Nephi proposed this: "The Lord God hath given a commandment that [everyone] should have charity, which charity is love" (2 Nephi 26:30).

President Russell M. Nelson taught that "each of us has a divine potential because each is a child of God. Each is equal in His eyes. The implications of this truth are profound. Brothers and sisters, please listen carefully to what I am about to say. God does not love one race more than another. His doctrine on this matter is clear. He invites *all* to come unto Him, 'black and white, bond and free, male and female.'" President Nelson further promised, "Your standing before God is not determined by the color of your skin. Favor or disfavor with God is dependent upon your devotion to God and His commandments and not the color of your skin." He called on all Latter-day Saints "to lead out in abandoning attitudes and actions of prejudice," and he pled with us "to promote respect for all of God's children."[27]

I love the way the Restoration solves problems, especially priesthood problems. I still have unanswered questions about the long history of race, priesthood, and temple. But I choose to hope and believe that the ongoing Restoration will resolve those problems because it has resolved so many others. I base that faith on knowledge. One thing I know is that President Kimball was a prophet of God who received revelation. This is how I know it: I was eight years old and at general conference in 1978 when the Saints accepted the revelation and sustained the revelator. Someone snapped a picture of my brother and me as we were about to shake President Kimball's hand outside the tabernacle after a session of conference.

What I remember most about that day, however, is how, as President Kimball entered the tabernacle, the Saints spontaneously arose and sang "We Thank Thee O God for a Prophet." I felt the

Holy Spirit overwhelm me during the singing. I raised my hand when President Tanner asked for a sustaining vote for Official Declaration 2—the testimony that revelation had been given, the long-promised day had come. I did not know what was at stake then. I did not know any of the relevant, verifiable facts, nor did I understand the eternal implications of the long-awaited, long-promised day. I had no idea how many people had hoped and prayed and pled for that day, including President Spencer W. Kimball. But I have studied all of that since. I have some understanding of it now.

This is what I know: I know by the overwhelming power of the Holy Ghost that Spencer W. Kimball was a prophet of God. He thought slowly. He sought and received a revelation that solved problems, made the fulfillment of the great commission and the gathering of covenant Israel possible, and reconciled the Church's original teachings with its current teachings. That revelation was sustained by all of the apostles and by the common consent of the Latter-day Saints in general conference. I know. I was there.

Epilogue
Why This Church Matters

The first revelation in the Doctrine and Covenants says that the Savior called and empowered Joseph Smith to "lay the foundation of this church, and to bring it forth out of obscurity and out of darkness, the only true and living church upon the face of the whole earth, with which I, the Lord am well pleased, speaking unto the church collectively and not individually" (Doctrine and Covenants 1:30). If you have made it this far in the book, you may not be able to think fast again when you or others testify, "I know this church is true." You will have to slow down.

You will find yourself asking questions like: What does it mean to know? What do I know? How do I know? What is the church? What does it mean that it is true? In what ways is it true? What does the Savior mean by *and* in Doctrine and Covenants 1:30? Does He want me to understand that His is the only true church *and* the only living church? Or does He mean that it is the only church that is both true *and* living at the same time? Or is it both? Or does He mean something else? Seeking answers to these kinds of questions by study of the best sources while exercising faith in Jesus Christ is a great way to spend a lifetime.

Here is what it means to me to say, as I delightedly do, *I know that The Church of Jesus Christ of Latter-day Saints is true*. It means that the Restoration is real. Christianity is being restored as we speak. Jesus is the Redeemer and the Restorer. He calls and qualifies flawed people to be prophets and apostles, Primary presidents and bishops, ministers and missionaries. It is a verifiable fact—regardless of one's point of view—that some prophets and apostles taught things that all of the Lord's living prophets and apostles now disavow. I have the power to interpret that fact however I want to, and I want to interpret it in a way that accounts best for *all* the verifiable facts, not isolated ones. Having considered other options, I have concluded that the best principles I can follow to guide my interpretation are faith, hope, and charity.

That leads me to these conclusions. My conviction that the Savior's church is true does not mean that I assume it is perfect. Elder J. Devn Cornish taught:

> It may seem reasonable to expect that the history of the true Church portray unerring leaders successfully implementing a sequence of revealed directions progressing to a perfect organization that is widely welcomed and embraced. But that is neither what the scriptures describe nor what our history represents, because the perfecting of the Church as an organization was not the Lord's primary purpose. Nowhere in our scriptures, our doctrine, or the teachings of latter-day apostles and prophets is it taught that the purpose of the

Lord is to perfect or to save the Church. Rather, the purpose of the Church is "for the perfecting of the saints . . . till we all come in the unity of the faith . . . unto a perfect man, unto the measure of the stature of the fulness of Christ" (Ephesians 4:12–13). The Lord's primary purpose is to perfect His Saints. The Church serves to support that objective.[1]

I do not interpret the word *perfecting* in that passage as flawless or mistake-free. The Greek word translated as *perfecting* conveys the idea of equipping or preparing, not flawlessness.[2] The Savior's church prepares Saints for the work of His ministry so we can all become finished—the meaning of the word translated as *perfect* in Ephesians 4:13. I try to remember what the Church is *of*—The Church *of* Jesus Christ *of* Latter-day Saints. It is composed of the perfect Christ along with imperfect Saints working together.

The restored scriptures tell us that we become perfect, finished, or completely created in God's image by being just and true—meaning obedient to God's law (including repentance) and faithful to our covenants with God. People who are faithful to their covenants to obey God's laws are "made perfect through Jesus the mediator of the new [or restored] covenant" (Doctrine and Covenants 76:69). I know that is true.

One way I know it is that everything changed for the better for me when I began believing it. I stopped believing the falsehood that I should be perfect so God could love me. I started to live the actual gospel, loving God because He sent His Beloved Son to perfect me—even me. Having made that mental shift—that conversion—covenants became the most important determinant of my daily life. That is because making and keeping covenants means getting in and staying in the healing and healthy relationship with God whereby He promises to perfect me through Christ. Faith in Jesus Christ came to life. I discovered the joy of daily repentance.[3] Renewing *covenants* regularly renewed *me*.

Along the way, I learned some scriptural math that is counter-cultural today but represents the restored gospel of Jesus Christ. The first truth, expressed in an equation is I = 0, meaning that I am nothing. Strange as it may seem, that is a comforting truth to accept for those of us who struggle with assuming that we are supposed to be perfect. We are not. We are nothing, as the scriptures clarify. The Book of Moses says that Moses talked with God and experienced His glory. Then Moses "was left unto himself. And as he was left unto himself, he fell unto the earth. . . . And he said unto himself: Now, for this cause I know that man is nothing, which thing I never had supposed" (Moses 1:9–10). That is not all. King Benjamin hoped his sermon would awaken his people "to a sense of your nothingness, and your worthless and fallen state," and he used that word *nothingness* twice (Mosiah 4:5, 11). Mormon piled on, saying, "O how great is the nothingness of the children of men; yea, even they are less than the dust of the earth" (Helaman 12:7). Ammon declared, "I know that I am nothing" (Alma 26:12). So do I. I = 0. I equal nothing. And so do you.

The good news is expressed in this equation: $I + \phi = \infty$. The symbol at the heart of the equation represents Jesus Christ. In Greek, the word *ichthys*, or fish, is also an acronym that many Christians use to stand for Jesus Christ, Son of God, Savior. So the fish symbolizes the Savior. The plus sign in the equation represents covenants. The infinity symbol at the end of the equation expresses what we are when we are in Christ: infinite. So $I + \phi = \infty$ expresses beautiful truths, including the power of the covenant by which we took upon ourselves the name of Jesus Christ. Without that covenant, that plus sign, that cross of Christ, we are on our own. And on our own we are nothing. God made us free to go our "own way" if that is what we choose (Doctrine and Covenants 1:16). But the gospel is "a more excellent way" (1 Corinthians 12:31). Jesus is that way (see Ether 12:11). Choosing to covenant with God to take upon ourselves the name of Jesus Christ—to become His, to add ourselves to Him—is the best possible way, the only way, to return to our heavenly parents and become like them.

Here is why: The scriptures say that it requires "an infinite and eternal sacrifice" to redeem a single soul—to take it from nothing to everything. Jacob said, "it must needs be an infinite atonement" (2 Nephi 9:7). Alma taught that "there can be nothing which is short of an infinite atonement which will suffice for the sins of the world" (Alma 34:12). Jesus Christ is the only one willing and able to make an infinite atonement. Nephi prophesied that Israelites would be scattered until they were persuaded "to believe in Christ, the Son of God, and the atonement, which is infinite for all mankind" (2 Nephi 25:16). Alma taught that the "great and last sacrifice will be the Son of God, yea, infinite and eternal. And thus he shall bring salvation to all those who shall believe on his name; . . . [or in other words, all who] have faith unto repentance. . . . for he is mighty to save" (Alma 34: 14–15, 18). Why did Jesus perform the infinite Atonement? Because, as Professor Truman Madsen explained, "If souls are of value in direct proportion to the concern and sacrifice of our Redeemer, then we know that in the eyes of the Father and the Son, your soul—even yours—and mine—even mine is of infinite worth."[4]

All of this means that though I = 0, I + Jesus Christ = infinity. Our nothingness plus His infinity equals infinity, and Jesus is infinite in every way. The scriptures say that He is infinitely glorious, powerful, truthful, just, and merciful. They say, in fact, that He has "an *infinity of fulness*, from everlasting to everlasting" (Doctrine and Covenants 109:77; emphasis added). When the Savior says, as He repeatedly does, "My grace is sufficient," He is making a radical understatement. We can choose to believe Him when He says his "grace is sufficient *for all*" (Ether 12:27; emphasis added), and when He says, "My grace is sufficient *for thee*" (2 Corinthians 12:9; emphasis added). When we covenant—when we choose to add Jesus Christ to our nothingness—then we can do all things through Christ. The instant we sincerely make the covenant to take upon ourselves the name of Jesus Christ, we become perfect in Christ.

The Church of Jesus Christ matters because it is His. He established it. He restored it. He commissioned it to tell the good news equation to all people everywhere. He empowered and authorized it to perform the ordinances in which people can covenant to add their nothingness to His infinite power to repent, His infinite forgiveness, and His infinite grace, giving us infinite opportunities to be redeemed, rescued, healed, helped, loved, and saved (see 2 Corinthians 12:7–10).

We cannot exhaust the Savior's infinity of fulness. There is enough for all of us to have all of Him. His grace is indeed sufficient. But here's the thing: That plus sign is up to each of us. And there is only one church in which we can add ourselves to Christ in the way and by the power He provided. If, like Joseph Smith, you want to be right "in matters that involve eternal consequences," then the Savior's church matters to you.[5] Depending on your tastes, there are churches with more exciting worship services, more skillful preaching, and other aspects worthy of holy envy. But only The Church of Jesus Christ of Latter-day Saints has the power and the commission—priesthood and keys—to perform the ordinances and make the covenants that endow us with God's power and seal us to Him and each other. Those covenants restore the relationship we once had. They empower us to regain God's presence. Moreover, they ensure that our most cherished relationships will transcend death and endure forever. No other church promises that. No other church has been empowered or commissioned to.

Even so, church can be hard. It is painful for many people, and not just because they wish, as I do, that they could express their joy in Jesus accompanied by an electric guitar and a drum set on the Sabbath. Some Saints have been abused by parents, leaders, or others in ways that make it difficult to dissociate the Savior's Church from their awful experiences at the hands of people who were supposed to be the Savior's disciples. Some Saints struggle with mixed messages and conflicting signals about how much they belong and are valued. All of that is verifiably true. So how might we choose to interpret it?

We can do what the Savior's Church is meant to do: We can love. We can minster to the body of Christ until we all come together. We can invite everyone to "join themselves to the Lord" by taking hold of His covenant. We can help "the Lord God which gathereth the outcasts of Israel" (Isaiah 56:8). We can follow the Lord's prophets. They know The Way. They call us to love rather than judge. They prescribed Jesus Christ as the answer to our problems and charity as the antidote to our ills, saying it "propels us 'to bear one another's burdens' rather than heap burdens upon each other."[6]

I choose to let the Savior's imperfect Church, led by flawed but actual, authorized apostles of the Lord Jesus Christ, point my fallen and flawed soul to Him. His restored gospel is the greatest good news there is. Covenants have made me and Him infinitely one. I know He can help and heal because He helps and heals me. You can know it too.

Acknowledgments

I gratefully acknowledge the many mentors and scholars whose work underpins everything in this book. I thank Janiece Johnson at Deseret Book for her wisdom and encouragement—not only in the preparation of this manuscript, but generally. I thank Kristen Evans and Tracy Keck because everyone needs at least one editor, and I needed two. As always with a book project, this one is so much better than it would have been if not for each person acknowledged above.

I debuted much of the content of this book—or meant to—on a tour of the sacred sites it mentions. Then I got sick at the Susquehanna River and left my friends in the lurch. I acknowledge, appreciate, and sincerely thank each of the friends and loved ones who went with me (geographically and empathetically) on that trip. I mean you, Carolyn. And Cherie and Kirk, Kristen and Kelly, Betty and Eugene and Juliann, Linda, JoAnn and Ron, Auburn ladies Sherry and Sheri and Frankie and Lynette, and Lauralyn and Steve, Helen and Roger, Judy and Bob, Celeste and Stephen, Jenny and

Colin and Janene, Ruth and Andrew, Emmaline, Lilian, Willa, and Benny. You all gave me so much more than you received. I am full of fondness for each of you. I am in your debt and at your service.

I especially thank and acknowledge Jenny Sebring. She encouraged my work on this book in all the usual ways, but this time while I wrote, she sculpted *Mother Love* and modeled for me how to infuse the creative process with revelation.

Notes

1. Think Slow

1. Daniel Kahneman, *Thinking Fast and Slow* (New York: Farrar, Straus and Giroux, 2011).
2. Journal, 1835–1836, The Joseph Smith Papers, 23, https://www.joseph smithpapers.org/paper-summary/journal-1835-1836/24.
3. "Scientists and Belief," 5 November 2009, Pew Research Center, https://www.pewresearch.org/religion/2009/11/05/scientists-and-belief/.
4. For a great example, see Jamie L. Jensen, "Faith and Science: Symbiotic Pathways to Truth," Brigham Young University Devotional, November 3, 2020, https://speeches.byu.edu/talks/jamie-jensen/faith-science-symbiotic-pathways-truth/.
5. Journal, 1835–1836, The Joseph Smith Papers, 23.

2. What Kind of a Being Is God?

1. Stephen H. Webb, *Mormon Christianity: What Other Christians Can Learn from the Latter-day Saints* (New York: Oxford University Press, 2013), 4–5; emphasis added.
2. Dallin H. Oaks, "Joseph Smith in a Personal World," in *The Worlds of Joseph Smith: A Bicentennial Conference at the Library of Congress*, ed. John W. Welch (Provo, UT: Brigham Young University Press, 2006), 167.

3. Russell M. Nelson, "Revelation for the Church, Revelation for Our Lives," *Ensign* or *Liahona*, May 2018.

4. James E. Faulconer, *Thinking Otherwise: Theological Explorations of Joseph Smith's Revelations* (Provo, UT: Neal A. Maxwell Institute for Religious Scholarship, 2020), 5–8.

5. Stephen J. Stein, "America's Bibles: Canon, Commentary, and Community," *Church History* 64 no. 2 (June 1995): 172.

6. Journal, December 1842–June 1844; Book 4, 1 March–22 June 1844, 65, The Joseph Smith Papers, https://www.josephsmithpapers.org/paper-summary/journal-december-1842-june-1844-book-4-1-march-22-june-1844/67.

7. See Lucy Mack Smith, History, 1845, 241, The Joseph Smith Papers, https://www.josephsmithpapers.org/paper-summary/lucy-mack-smith-history-1845/249; April 28, 1842 • Thursday, *The First Fifty Years of Relief Society*, https://www.churchhistorianspress.org/the-first-fifty-years-of-relief-society/part-1/1-2/1-2-7; and Discourse, 9 April 1842, as reported by Wilford Woodruff, The Joseph Smith Papers, https://www.josephsmithpapers.org/paper-summary/discourse-9-april-1842-as-reported-by-wilford-woodruff/1#facts.

8. Discourse, 7 April 1844, as Reported by Wilford Woodruff, 133, The Joseph Smith Papers, https://www.josephsmithpapers.org/paper-summary/discourse-7-april-1844-as-reported-by-wilford-woodruff/1.

9. See Daniel Kahneman, *Thinking Fast and Slow* (New York: Farrar, Straus and Giroux, 2011).

10. Richard D. Draper and Michael D. Rhodes, *Epistle to the Hebrews* (Provo, UT: BYU Studies, 2021), 181.

11. Draper and Rhodes, *Epistle to the Hebrews*, 181–182; emphasis added.

12. Discourse, 7 April 1844, as Reported by Wilford Woodruff, 135.

13. Discourse, 7 April 1844, as Reported by Wilford Woodruff, 136.

14. Discourse, 7 April 1844, as Reported by Wilford Woodruff, 137.

15. Dallin H. Oaks, "Apostasy and Restoration," *Ensign*, May 1995. Also quoted in Gospel Topics, "Mother in Heaven," topics.ChurchofJesusChrist.org.

16. Stephen H. Webb, *Mormon Christianity: What Other Christians Can Learn from the Latter-day Saints* (New York: Oxford University Press, 2013), 8–9.

3. A Family Ready for Restoration

1. Jonathan Edwards, "Personal Narrative," in *The Works of Jonathan Edwards* vol. 16, ed. Perry Miller, John E. Smith, Harry S. Stout (New Haven: Yale University Press, 1957), 791–793, as cited in George M. Marsden, *Jonathan Edwards: A Life* (New Haven: Yale University Press, 2003), 40–43.

2. Jonathan Edwards, "On Sarah Pierpont," in *The Works of Jonathan Edwards* vol. 16, ed. Perry Miller, John E. Smith, Harry S. Stout (New Haven: Yale University Press, 1957), 789–790.

3. George M. Marsden, *Johathan Edwards: A Life* (New Haven: Yale University Press, 2003), 249–252.

4. Jonathan Edwards, "Sinners in the Hands of an Angry God," in *The Works of Jonathan Edwards* vol. 22, ed. Perry Miller, John E. Smith, Harry S. Stout (New Haven: Yale University Press, 1957).

5. Terryl L. Givens, "Lightning Out of Heaven: Joseph Smith and the Forging of Community," *BYU Studies Quarterly* 45 no. 1 (2006): 10.

6. Letter, 1799 April 10, MS 1139, Church History Library, The Church of Jesus Christ of Latter-day Saints, Salt Lake City, https://catalog.churchof jesuschrist.org/assets/27a0e33f-be48-44a9-82b7-21f0cf5e03b4/0/0.

7. Lucy Mack Smith, History, 1845, 48–52, The Joseph Smith Papers, https:// www.josephsmithpapers.org/paper-summary/lucy-mack-smith-history -1845/57.

4. Joseph's Head and Heart Dilemma

1. History, circa Summer 1832, The Joseph Smith Papers, https://www .josephsmithpapers.org/paper-summary/history-circa-summer-1832 /1#full-transcript.

2. Alexander Neibaur, Journal, 24 May 1844, extract, 23, The Joseph Smith Papers, https://www.josephsmithpapers.org/paper-summary/alexander -neibaur-journal-24-may-1844-extract/1.

3. "Joseph Smith's First Prayer," *Hymns*, no. 26.

5. First Vision Accounts

1. Jeffrey R. Holland, "'Lord, I Believe,'" *Ensign* or *Liahona*, May 2013.

2. David Hackett Fischer, *Historians' Fallacies: Toward a Logic of Historical Thought* (New York: Harper Perennial, 1970), 24.

3. Dan Vogel, *Joseph Smith: The Making of a Prophet* (Salt Lake City: Signature, 2004), xv.

4. Ann Taves and Steven C. Harper, "Joseph Smith's First Vision: New Methods for the Analysis of Experience-Related Texts," *Mormon Studies Review* 3 (2016): 53–84. See also Ann Taves, "First Vision Controversies," *BYU Studies Quarterly* 59 no. 2 (2020).

5. Stephen Prothero, *American Jesus: How the Son of God Became a National Icon* (New York: Farrar, Straus and Giroux, 2003), 171.

6. Joseph's Other Dilemma

1. Letter to Emma Smith, 6 June 1832, 1, The Joseph Smith Papers, https://www.josephsmithpapers.org/paper-summary/letter-to-emma-smith-6-june-1832/1.

2. History, 1838–1856, volume A-1 [23 December 1805–30 August 1834], 4, The Joseph Smith Papers, https://www.josephsmithpapers.org/paper-summary/history-1838-1856-volume-a-1-23-december-1805-30-august-1834/4.

3. History, circa Summer 1832, The Joseph Smith Papers, https://www.josephsmithpapers.org/paper-summary/history-circa-summer-1832/1.

7. Source Criticism

1. History, circa Summer 1832, The Joseph Smith Papers, https://www.josephsmithpapers.org/paper-summary/history-circa-summer-1832/1.

2. Journal, 1835–1836, The Joseph Smith Papers, https://www.josephsmithpapers.org/paper-summary/journal-1835-1836/24?p=24.

3. Church History, 1 March 1842, The Joseph Smith Papers, https://www.josephsmithpapers.org/paper-summary/church-history-1-march-1842/1?p=1.

4. Appendix: Orson Pratt, *A[n] Interesting Account of Several Remarkable Visions,* 1840, The Joseph Smith Papers, https://www.josephsmithpapers.org/paper-summary/appendix-orson-pratt-an-interesting-account-of-several-remarkable-visions-1840/3?p=3.

5. Orson Hyde, *Ein Ruf aus der Wüste* (A Cry out of the Wilderness), 1842, extract, English translation, The Joseph Smith Papers, https://www.josephsmithpapers.org/paper-summary/orson-hyde-ein-ruf-aus-der-wste-a-cry-out-of-the-wilderness-1842-extract-english-translation/1.

6. Levi Richards, Journal, 11 June 1843, extract, The Joseph Smith Papers,

https://www.josephsmithpapers.org/paper-summary/levi-richards-journal
-11-june-1843-extract/1.

7. Interview, 29 August 1843, Extract, The Joseph Smith Papers, https://www
.josephsmithpapers.org/paper-summary/interview-29-august-1843
-extract/1.

8. History, 1838–1856, volume A-1 [23 December 1805–30 August
1834], 4, The Joseph Smith Papers, https://www.josephsmithpapers.org
/paper-summary/history-1838-1856-volume-a-1-23-december-1805-30
-august-1834/575.

9. History, circa Summer 1832.

10. History, circa Summer 1832.

11. History, circa June 1839–circa 1841 [Draft 2].

12. "Church History," 1 March 1842.

13. Journal, 1835–1836.

14. Interview, 29 August 1843, Extract.

15. Alexander Neibaur, Journal, 24 May 1844, extract, The Joseph Smith Papers,
https://www.josephsmithpapers.org/paper-summary/alexander-neibaur
-journal-24-may-1844-extract/1.

16. Journal, 1835–1836.

17. John W. Welch, editor, *Opening the Heavens: Accounts of Divine Manifestations, 1820–1844* 2nd ed. (Provo, UT: BYU Studies, 2017), 67, fn. 38.

18. "Church History," 1 March 1842.

19. Levi Richards, Journal, 11 June 1843, extract.

8. A Teenage Seer

1. History, circa Summer 1832, 3, The Joseph Smith Papers, https://www
.josephsmithpapers.org/paper-summary/history-circa-summer-1832/3.

2. History, circa Summer 1832, 3–4.

3. Journal, 1835–1836, 24, The Joseph Smith Papers, https://www.joseph
smithpapers.org/paper-summary/journal-1835-1836/25.

4. Karen Lynn Davidson, David J. Whittaker, Mark Ashurst-McGee, and
Richard L. Jensen, eds., *The Joseph Smith Papers, Histories, Volume 1: 1832–
1844* (Salt Lake City: Church Historian's Press, 2012), 14.

5. History, 1838–1856, volume A-1 [23 December 1805–30 August 1834],
The Joseph Smith Papers, https://www.josephsmithpapers.org/paper
-summary/history-1838-1856-volume-a-1-23-december-1805-30
-august-1834/575.

6. Lucy Mack Smith, History, 1845, 85, The Joseph Smith Papers, https://www.josephsmithpapers.org/paper-summary/lucy-mack-smith-history-1845/92.

7. Appendix: Reminiscence of William D. Purple, 28 April 1877 [*State of New York v. JS–A*], The Joseph Smith Papers, https://www.josephsmithpapers.org/paper-summary/appendix-reminiscence-of-william-d-purple-28-april-1877-state-of-new-york-v-js-a/1.

8. Appendix: Reminiscence of William D. Purple, 28 April 1877.

9. The Joseph Smith Papers published the agreement between Josiah Stowell, Joseph Smith Sen, Joseph Smith Jr, and others to share any treasure they discovered. Appendix 1: Agreement of Josiah Stowell and Others, 1 November 1825, 4, The Joseph Smith Papers, https://www.josephsmithpapers.org/paper-summary/appendix-1-agreement-of-josiah-stowell-and-others-1-november-1825/1.

10. Geoffrey Crayon, Gent. [Washington Irvine], *Tales of a Traveller*, (Philadelphia: H. C. Cary & I. Lee, Chestnut-Street, 1824), https://www.gutenberg.org/files/13514/13514-h/13514-h.htm#part04.

11. Lucy Mack Smith, History, 1845, The Joseph Smith Papers, https://www.josephsmithpapers.org/paper-summary/lucy-mack-smith-history-1845/102; emphasis added.

12. "Appendix: Reminiscence of William D. Purple, 28 April 1877.

13. "Mormonism," *Tiffany* 5 (August 1859): 163–164, https://archive.org/details/threewitnesses/page/n23/mode/1up?view=theater.

14. "Tabernacle," *Deseret News* 10 no. 43 (December 26, 1860), https://newspapers.lib.utah.edu/details?id=2585868.

15. Dallin H. Oaks, "Recent Events Involving Church History and Forged Documents," *Ensign*, October 1987.

9. Two Problems of Book of Mormon Translation

1. History, circa Summer 1832, 5, The Joseph Smith Papers, https://www.josephsmithpapers.org/paper-summary/history-circa-summer-1832/5.

2. History, circa Summer 1832.

3. Preface to the Book of Mormon, circa August 1829, The Joseph Smith Papers, https://www.josephsmithpapers.org/paper-summary/preface-to-book-of-mormon-circa-august-1829/1.

4. Minutes, 25–26 October 1831, 13, The Joseph Smith Papers, https://www.josephsmithpapers.org/paper-summary/minutes-25-26-october-1831/4.

5. Lucy Mack Smith, History, 1845, The Joseph Smith Papers, https://www.josephsmithpapers.org/paper-summary/lucy-mack-smith-history-1845/102.

6. "A Peaceful Heart," *The Friend*, September 1974, https://www.churchofjesuschrist.org/study/friend/1974/09/a-peaceful-heart? lang=eng.

7. Original Manuscript of the Book of Mormon, circa 12 April 1828–circa 1 July 1829, 3, The Joseph Smith Papers, https://www.josephsmithpapers.org/paper-summary/original-manuscript-of-the-book-of-mormon-circa-12-april-1828-circa-1-july-1829/1. See also Printer's Manuscript of the Book of Mormon, circa August 1829–circa January 1830, i, The Joseph Smith Papers, https://www.josephsmithpapers.org/paper-summary/printers-manuscript-of-the-book-of-mormon-circa-august-1829-circa-january-1830/1.

8. John W. Welch, editor, *Opening the Heavens: Accounts of Divine Manifestations, 1820–1844* (Provo, UT: BYU Studies; Salt Lake City: Deseret Book, 2005), 76–213, https://byustudies.byu.edu/online-chapters/documents-of-the-translation-of-the-book-of-mormon/.

9. "Church History," 1 March 1842, 707, The Joseph Smith Papers, https://www.josephsmithpapers.org/paper-summary/church-history-1-march-1842/2.

10. Edmund C. Briggs, "A Visit to Nauvoo in 1856," *Journal of History* (October 1916): 454.

11. "One of the Three Witnesses: Incidents in the Life of Martin Harris," *Millennial Star* 44 no. 8, (1882): 87.

12. *Latter-day Saints' Messenger and Advocate* 1 (October 1834), 14–16.

13. Reuben Miller, journal, 1848–1849, MS 1392, Church History Library, The Church of Jesus Christ of Latter-day Saints, Salt Lake City, https://catalog.churchofjesuschrist.org/record/0448e354-d892-4ea7-9e2a-28b714114909/22222322-f4fe-41e3-aa86-bfc54b94df92?.

14. "Documents of the Translation of the Book of Mormon," *Opening the Heavens: Accounts of Divine Manifestations 1820–1844*, ed. John Welch, (Provo, UT: BYU Studies; Salt Lake City: Deseret Book, 2005), https://byustudies.byu.edu/wp-content/uploads/2020/11/chp-welch-opening-2-sec2.pdf.

10. Another Problem of Book of Mormon Translation

1. Brian C. Hales, "Naturalistic Explanations of the Origin of the Book of Mormon: A Longitudinal Study," *BYU Studies Quarterly* 58 no. 3 (2019): 105–148.

2. "Last Testimony of Sister Emma," *Saint's Herald* 26 no. 19 (1 October 1879): 289, https://archive.org/details/TheSaintsHerald_Volume_26_1879/page/n287/mode/2up?view=theater.

3. The statement repeatedly denies that Joseph received a revelation regarding plural marriage, or ever practiced it, or that Emma knew anything about it. Some people credit these statements as true, but verifiable evidence shows that they are not. For orientation to this evidence and its misinterpretation, see Brian Hales's website, josephsmithspolygamy.org, and his video, "Denver Snuffer: Polygamy Reductionist and Non-Transparencyist," www.youtube.com/watch?v=ZpxbfPCP2b8.

4. See Edmund C. Briggs, "A Visit to Nauvoo in 1856," *Journal of History* (October 1916): 454.

5. ohineedascreenname, "Emma quote about Joseph's translating ability," Reddit post, https://www.reddit.com/r/mormon/comments/r6tdsv/emma_quote_about_josephs_translating_ability/.

6. See David Hackett Fischer, *Historians' Fallacies: Toward a Logic of Historical Thought* (New York: Harper Perennial, 1970), 24.

7. Brian C. Hales, "Naturalistic Explanations of the Origin of the Book of Mormon," *BYU Studies Quarterly*.

8. Lucy Mack Smith, History, 1844–1845, The Joseph Smith Papers, https://www.josephsmithpapers.org/paper-summary/lucy-mack-smith-history-1844-1845/43.

9. Letter to Oliver Cowdery, 22 October 1829, 9, The Joseph Smith Papers, https://www.josephsmithpapers.org/paper-summary/letter-to-oliver-cowdery-22-october-1829/1#source-note. Letter to the Church in Colesville, 2 December 1830, 196, The Joseph Smith Papers, https://www.josephsmithpapers.org/paper-summary/letter-to-the-church-in-colesville-2-december-1830/1#source-note.

10. Letter to Martin Harris, 22 February 1831, 1, The Joseph Smith Papers, https://www.josephsmithpapers.org/paper-summary/letter-to-martin-harris-22-february-1831/1#source-note. Letter to Hyrum Smith, 3–4 March

1831, 2, The Joseph Smith Papers, https://www.josephsmithpapers.org/paper-summary/letter-to-hyrum-smith-3-4-march-1831/2.

11. Letter to Emma Smith, 6 June 1832, 1, The Joseph Smith Papers, https://www.josephsmithpapers.org/paper-summary/letter-to-emma-smith-6-june-1832/1.

12. Letter to William W. Phelps, 27 November 1832, 2, The Joseph Smith Papers, https://www.josephsmithpapers.org/paper-summary/letter-to-william-w-phelps-27-november-1832/2.

13. See Janiece L. Johnson, "'Give It All Up and Follow Your Lord': Mormon Female Religiosity, 1831–1843" (MA thesis, Brigham Young University, 2001), 58–63.

14. Janiece L. Johnson, "'The Scripture Is a Fulfilling': Sally Parker's Weave," *BYU Studies Quarterly* 44 no. 2 (2005): 116, https://archive.bookofmormoncentral.org/content/scripture-fulfilling-sally-parkers-weave.

15. Johnson, "'The Scriptures Is a Fulfilling': Sally Parker's Weave."

16. Jan Shipps and John W. Welch, editors, *The Journals of William E. McLellin, 1831–1836* (Provo, UT: BYU Studies and Urbana, IL: University of Illinois, 1994), 33.

17. Mitchell K. Schaefer, editor, *William McLellin's Lost Manuscript* (Salt Lake City: Eborn, 2012), 165–167.

18. Mitchell K. Schaefer, "'The Testimony of Men': William E. McLellin and the Book of Mormon Witnesses," *BYU Studies Quarterly* 50 no. 1 (2011): 99–110.

19. Schaefer, "'The Testimony of Men.'"

20. William E. McLellin to James T. Cobb, Independence, Missouri, August 14, 1880, Manuscripts Collection, New York Public Library, in *The William E. McLellin Papers, 1854–1880*, ed. Stan Larson and Samuel J. Passey (Salt Lake City: Signature Books, 2007), 521–23.

21. William E. McLellin to James T. Cobb, Independence, Missouri, August 14, 1880.

11. Another Testament of Jesus Christ

1. History, 1838–1856, volume A-1 [23 December 1805–30 August 1834], 34, The Joseph Smith Papers, https://www.josephsmithpapers.org/paper-summary/history-1838-1856-volume-a-1-23-december-1805-30-august-1834/40.

2. Mark Twain, *Roughing It* (New York: Signet, 2008).

3. See Janiece L. Johnson, "'Give It All Up and Follow Your Lord': Mormon Female Religiosity, 1831–1843" (MA thesis, Brigham Young University, 2001), 151–155. Lyndon W. Cook, "'I Have Sinned Against Heaven, and Am Unworthy of Your Confidence, But I Cannot Live without a Reconciliation': Thomas B. Marsh Returns to the Church," *BYU Studies Quarterly* 20 no. 4 (1980): 389–400.

4. See Johnson, "'Give It All Up and Follow Your Lord': Mormon Female Religiosity, 1831–1843."

12. How the Restoration Resolves Priesthood Problems

1. Richard Scot to Friends, no date, in George Fox, *A New-England Fire-Brand Quenched* (London, 1678), 247, https://www.proquest.com/eebo /docview/2240954359/pageLevelImage?imgSeq=258&sourcetype=Books &imgSeq=259.

2. W. Clark Gilpin, *The Millenarian Piety of Roger Williams* (Chicago: University of Chicago Press, 1979), 59.

3. Russell M. Nelson, "The Atonement," *Ensign*, November 1996.

4. See Steven C. Harper, "Oliver Cowdery as Second Witness of Priesthood Restoration," in *Days Never to Be Forgotten: Oliver Cowdery*, edited by Alexander L. Baugh, (Salt Lake City: Deseret Book, 2009), https://rsc.byu .edu/days-never-be-forgotten-oliver-cowdery/oliver-cowdery-second -witness-priesthood-restoration.

5. "Before 8 August 1839" in *The Words of Joseph Smith: The Contemporary Accounts of the Nauvoo Discourses of the Prophet Joseph*, edited by Andrew F. Ehat and Lyndon W. Cook (Salt Lake City: Bookcraft, 1980), https://rsc .byu.edu/words-joseph-smith/before-8-august-1839-1.

6. Letter to the Church, 7 September 1842 [D&C 128], 7, The Joseph Smith Papers, https://www.josephsmithpapers.org/paper-summary/letter-to-the -church-7-september-1842-dc-128/7.

7. Minute Book 1, 159, The Joseph Smith Papers, https://www.josephsmith papers.org/paper-summary/minute-book-1/163.

8. History, 1838–1856, volume A-1 [23 December 1805–30 August 1834], 26, The Joseph Smith Papers, https://www.josephsmithpapers.org/paper -summary/history-1838-1856-volume-a-1-23-december-1805-30-august -1834/32.

9. History, 1838–1856, volume A-1 [23 December 1805–30 August 1834], 27.

13. William McLellin's Love/Hate Relationship with Revelation

1. David A. Bednar, "The Spirit of Revelation," *Ensign* or *Liahona*, May 2011.

2. David Carpenter, "Revelation in Comparative Perspective: Lessons for Interreligious Dialogue," *Journal of Ecumenical Studies* 29, no. 2 (Spring 1992): 185–86.

3. Jan Shipps and John W. Welch, editors, *The Journals of William E. McLellin, 1831–1836* (Provo, UT: BYU Studies and Urbana, IL: University of Illinois, 1994), 29.

4. William E. McLellin, Journal 1, July 18–Nov 20, 1831, Church History Library, The Church of Jesus Christ of Latter-day Saints, Salt Lake City, https://catalog.churchofjesuschrist.org/record/c07ecf6a-0ac3-44a5-8a2e-aabab907c601/98619acf-7861-4f74-bf93-019e4b88051d?view=browse&lang=eng.

5. William E. McLellin, Journal 1, July 18–Nov 20, 1831.

6. Letterbook 1, 4, The Joseph Smith Papers, https://www.josephsmithpapers.org/paper-summa.

7. Letter to William W. Phelps, 27 November 1832, 4, The Joseph Smith Papers, https://www.josephsmithpapers.org/paper-summary/letter-to-william-w-phelps-27-november-1832/4.

8. History, 1838–1856, volume A-1 [23 December 1805–30 August 1834], 161, The Joseph Smith Papers, https://www.josephsmithpapers.org/paper-summary/history-1838-1856-volume-a-1-23-december-1805-30-august-1834/167.

9. Minute Book 2, 18, The Joseph Smith Papers, https://www.josephsmithpapers.org/paper-summary/minute-book-2/20.

10. Minute Book 2, 11.

11. History, 1838–1856, volume A-1 [23 December 1805–30 August 1834], 162.

12. History, 1838–1856, volume A-1.

13. Minute Book 2, 16.

14. Testimony, circa 2 November 1831, 121, The Joseph Smith Papers, https://www.josephsmithpapers.org/paper-summary/testimony-circa-2-november-1831/1.

15. Russell M. Nelson, "Revelation for the Church, Revelation for Our Lives," *Ensign* or *Liahona*, May 2018.

16. Minutes, 8 November 1831, 16, The Joseph Smith Papers, https://www
    .josephsmithpapers.org/paper-summary/minutes-8-november-1831/1.

17. Letter to William W. Phelps, 31 July 1832, 5, The Joseph Smith Papers,
    https://www.josephsmithpapers.org/paper-summary/letter-to-william-w
    -phelps-31-july-1832/5.

18. Oliver Cowdery, *The Evening and Morning Star,* 1835; repr., Burlington,
    WI: n.p., 1992, 16.

19. If you are interested, see Grant Underwood, "'The Laws of the Church
    of Christ' (D&C 42): A Textual and Historical Analysis," in *The Doctrine
    and Covenants: Revelations in Context,* edited by Andrew H. Hedges,
    J. Spencer Fluhman, and Alonzo L. Gaskill (Provo, UT: Religious Studies
    Center; Salt Lake City: Deseret Book, 2008), 108–141. Steven C. Harper,
    "'That They Might Come to Understanding': Revelation as Process," in
    You Shall Have My Word: Exploring the Text of the Doctrine and Covenants,
    edited by Scott C. Esplin, Richard O. Cowan, and Rachel Cope (Provo,
    UT: Religious Studies Center; Salt Lake City: Deseret Book, 2012), 19–
    33. And if you are really, really interested, see Robert J. Woodford, "The
    Historical Development of the Doctrine and Covenants," 3 volumes, PhD
    dissertation, Brigham Young University, 1974, https://archive.org/details
    /HistoricalDevelopmentOfTheDoctrineAndCovenants/page/n3/mode/2up.

20. William E. McLellin to relatives, August 1832, in *Journals of William E.
    McLellin, 1831–1836,* edited by Jan Shipps and John Welch (Provo, UT:
    BYU Studies, 1994), 79–84.

21. Letter to Emma Smith, 6 June 1832, 2, The Joseph Smith Papers, https://
    www.josephsmithpapers.org/paper-summary/letter-to-emma-smith-6-june
    -1832/2.

22. *Journals of William E. McLellin,* 229–230.

23. Journal, March–September 1838, 41, The Joseph Smith Papers, https://
    www.josephsmithpapers.org/paper-summary/journal-march-september
    -1838/27#16721676762174668782.

24. History, 1838–1856, volume A-1 [23 December 1805–30 August 1834],
    162. Letterbook 1, 4.

25. Stan Larson and Samuel J. Passey, editors, *The William E. McLellin Papers
    1854–1880* (Salt Lake City: Signature Books, 2008), 474–75; Robin Scott
    Jensen, Robert J. Woodford, and Steven C. Harper, editors, *The Joseph
    Smith Papers, Revelations and Translations, Manuscript Revelation Books* (Salt
    Lake City: Church Historian's Press, 2009), xxix.

26. Brigham Young, in *Journal of Discourses* volume 2, (Liverpool: F. D. Richards; London: Latter-day Saints' Book Depot, 1855), 314.
27. See David A. Bednar, "The Spirit of Revelation."

14. Reading the Bible Like Joseph Smith Did

1. History, 1838–1856, volume A-1 [23 December 1805–30 August 1834], 2, The Joseph Smith Papers, https://www.josephsmithpapers.org/paper-summary/history-1838-1856-volume-a-1-23-december-1805-30-august-1834/2.
2. Elders' Journal, July 1838, 43, The Joseph Smith Papers, https://www.josephsmithpapers.org/paper-summary/elders-journal-july-1838/11.
3. "The Westminster Confession of Faith," Ligonier.org, https://www.ligonier.org/learn/articles/westminster-confession-faith.
4. After revealing a lot of vital truth while working through Genesis, Exodus, and Deuteronomy, Joseph had less to say about the rest of the Old Testament. He said nothing about Ecclesiastes, which says almost nothing about God. When he got to the erotic poetry in the Song of Solomon, Joseph noted, "The Songs of Solomon are not Inspired writings." Old Testament Revision 2, 97, The Joseph Smith Papers, https://www.josephsmithpapers.org/paper-summary/old-testament-revision-2/104.
5. Jared. W. Ludlow, "The Joseph Smith Translation of the Bible: Ancient Material Restored or Inspired Commentary? Canonical or Optional? Finished or Unfinished?," *BYU Studies Quarterly* 60 no. 3 (2021): 147–158.

15. Scrolls, Mummies, and the Book of Abraham

1. Historical Department journal history of the Church, 1830–2008; 1830–1839; 1835; Church History Library, The Church of Jesus Christ of Latter-day Saints, Salt Lake City, https://catalog.churchofjesuschrist.org/assets/19f871d7-9f8b-414b-9a93-2fae5e62e8cd/0/259.
2. John Whitmer, History, 1831–circa 1847, The Joseph Smith Papers, https://www.josephsmithpapers.org/paper-summary/john-whitmer-history-1831-circa-1847/1.
3. "How Did Joseph Smith Translate the Book of Abraham?," Pearl of Great Price Central, January 30, 2020, https://pearlofgreatpricecentral.org/how-did-joseph-smith-translate-the-book-of-abraham/#_sup20.
4. Discourse, 16 June 1844–A, as Reported by Thomas Bullock, 3, The

Joseph Smith Papers, https://www.josephsmithpapers.org/paper-summary /iscourse-16-june-1844-a-as-reported-by-thomas-bullock/3.

5. Charlotte Haven, Letter, March 5, 1843; rep. "A Girl's Letters from Nauvoo," *Overland Monthly* 16, no. 96 (December 1890): 623–624.

6. Gospel Topics, "Translation and Historicity of the Book of Abraham," topics .ChurchofJesusChrist.org.

7. Michael MacKay and Daniel Belnap, "The Pure Language Project," *Journal of Mormon History* 49 no. 4 (2023): 43.

8. Account of Meeting and Discourse, 5 January 1841, as Reported by William P. McIntire, p. 1, The Joseph Smith Papers, https://www.josephsmith papers.org/paper-summary/account-of-meeting-and-discourse-5-january -1841-as-reported-by-william-p-mcintire/1.

9. Account of Meeting and Discourses, circa 9 March 1841, 14, The Joseph Smith Papers, https://www.josephsmithpapers.org/paper-summary /account-of-meeting-and-discourses-circa-9march-1841/1.

16. How Restored Priesthood Keys Solve the Soteriological Problem

1. Douglas J. Davies, *An Introduction to Mormonism* (Cambridge, UK: Cambridge University Press, 2010).

2. William W. Phelps to Sally Waterman Phelps, January 1836, L. Tom Perry Special Collections, Harold B. Lee Library, Brigham Young University, Provo, UT.

3. For examples, see jessehurlbut.net and search for "harrowing." Also see David L. Paulsen, Roger D. Cook, and Kendel J. Christensen, "The Harrowing of Hell: Salvation for the Dead in Early Christianity," *Journal of Book of Mormon Studies* 19 no. 1 (2010): 56–77.

4. David L. Paulsen and Brent Alvord, "Joseph Smith and the Problem of the Unevangelized," *Review of Books on the Book of Mormon 1989–2011* 17 no. 1 (2005): 171–204.

5. *Messenger and Advocate* 2 (March 1836): 274–81, available on "Mormon Publications: 19th and 20th Centuries," *BYU Harold B. Lee Library Digital Collections,* http://contentdm.lib.byu.edu/cdm/ref/collection/NCMP1820 -1846/id/7229.

6. *Messenger and Advocate* 2 (March 1836): 274–81.

7. Journal, 1835–1836, 192, The Joseph Smith Papers, https://www.joseph smithpapers.org/paper-summary/journal-1835-1836/195.

8. See "The Spirit of God," *Hymns,* no. 2.

9. This is known primarily from a pair of documents: Revelation, 12 January 1838–C, 1, The Joseph Smith Papers, https://www.josephsmithpapers.org /paper-summary/revelation-12-january-1838-c/1 and Lucy Mack Smith, History, 1845, 241, The Joseph Smith Papers, https://www.josephsmith papers.org/paper-summary/lucy-mack-smith-history-1845/249.

17. Harriet Brunson, Jane Neyman, and Baptism for the Dead

1. This is known primarily from a pair of documents: Revelation, 12 January 1838–C, 1, The Joseph Smith Papers, https://www.josephsmithpapers.org /paper-summary/revelation-12-january-1838-c/1 and Lucy Mack Smith, History, 1845, 241, The Joseph Smith Papers, https://www.josephsmith papers.org/paper-summary/lucy-mack-smith-history-1845/249.

2. Simon Baker, statement, in Journal History, August 15, 1840, quoted in *The Words of Joseph Smith*, edited by Andrew F. Ehat and Lyndon W. Cook (Provo, UT: Religious Studies Center, 1980), 49 note 1.

3. Joseph Smith to the Twelve, October 19, 1840, Manuscript History of the Church, vol. C–1, 1118, https://www.josephsmithpapers.org/paper -summary/history-1838-1856-volume-c-1-2-november-1838-31-july -1842/427.

4. Nauvoo Relief Society Minute Book, 83, The Joseph Smith Papers, https:// www.josephsmithpapers.org/paper-summary/nauvoo-relief-society-minute -book/106.

5. Letter to "All the Saints in Nauvoo," 1 September 1842 [D&C 127], 2, The Joseph Smith Papers, https://www.josephsmithpapers.org/paper-summary /letter-to-all-the-saints-in-nauvoo-1-september-1842-dc-127/2.

6. Speech Delivered by President B. Young, in the City of Joseph, April 6, 1845, *Times and Seasons* 6 no. 12 (July 1, 1845): 953.

18. Relief Society, Masonry, and the Endowment of Power

1. Joseph Smith, quoted in Sarah Granger Kimball, "Auto-biography," *Woman's Exponent*, Sept. 1, 1883, 52. In another version of the story, Sarah Granger Kimball remembered what Joseph told Eliza as, "I want you to tell the sisters . . . that their offering is accepted of the Lord and will result in a blessing to them," he said. But "this is not what the sisters want, there is something better for them. I have desired to organize the sisters in the order of the Priesthood. I now have the key by which I can do it." Or, alter-natively, Joseph asked Eliza to have the sisters "meet with me and a few of

the brethren in the Masonic Hall on Thursday at 1 P.M. next, and I will organise you in the Order of the Priesthood after the pattern of the Church." See Sarah M. Kimball, "Reminiscence," March 17, 1882, *National Women's Relief Society Record, 1880–1892*, Church History Library, The Church of Jesus Christ of Latter-day Saints, Salt Lake City.

2. Jeni Broberg Holzapfel and Richard Nietzel Holzapfel, eds., *A Woman's View: Helen Mar Whitney's Reminiscences of Early Church History* (Provo, UT: Religious Studies Center, 1997), 79–81.

3. Much of the literature about Freemasonry is marred by partisanship—for or against—or is speculative and unsound. Recently, however, good scholarship on the topic has begun to flourish. A sound introduction to Freemasonry is Margaret C. Jacob, *The Origins of Freemasonry: Facts and Fictions* (Philadelphia: University of Pennsylvania Press, 2006), 92–129. For Freemasonry in its American context, see Steven C. Bullock, *Revolutionary Brotherhood: Freemasonry and the Transformation of the American Social Order, 1730–1840* (Chapel Hill: University of North Carolina Press, 1996). The most thorough study of the relationships between Masonry and Mormonism is Michael W. Homer, *Joseph's Temples: The Dynamic Relationship Between Freemasonry and Mormonism* (Salt Lake City: University of Utah Press, 2014). Also relevant is Richard L. Bushman, *Joseph Smith: Rough Stone Rolling* (New York: Alfred A. Knopf, 2005), 450. See also Mark C. Carnes, *Secret Ritual and Manhood in Victorian America* (New Haven: Yale University Press, 1989), 110, and Steven Epperson, "'The Grand, Fundamental Principle': Joseph Smith and the Virtue of Friendship," *Journal of Mormon History* 23, no. 2 (Fall 1997): 78–80.

4. Jeni Broberg Holzapfel and Richard Neitzel Holzapfel, eds., *A Woman's View: Helen Mar Whitney's Reminiscences of Early Church History* (Salt Lake City: Deseret Book, 2011), 79–81. For context, see Stanley B. Kimball, *Heber C. Kimball: Mormon Patriarch and Pioneer* (Urbana, IL: University of Illinois Press, 1981), 12–13.

5. Heber C. Kimball, "Synopsis of the History of Heber Chase Kimball," *Deseret News* 8, no. 4 (March 31, 1858): 25.

6. Journal, December 1841–December 1842, 91, The Joseph Smith Papers, https://www.josephsmithpapers.org/paper-summary/journal-december -1841-december-1842/22.

7. Heber C. Kimball, Journal 92, April 10, 1845, Church History Library, The Church of Jesus Christ of Latter-day Saints, Salt Lake City.

8. Nauvoo Relief Society Minute Book, 4, The Joseph Smith Papers, https://www.josephsmithpapers.org/paper-summary/nauvoo-relief-society-minute-book/27.

9. Joseph Smith, Discourses to Nauvoo Female Relief Society, March 31 and April 28, 1842, as Revised for "History of Joseph Smith," September 5 and 19, 1855, *The First Fifty Years of Relief Society*, https://churchhistorianspress.org/the-first-fifty-years-of-relief-society/part-2/2-2.

10. April 28, 1842 • Thursday, *The First Fifty Years of Relief Society*, https://churchhistorianspress.org/the-first-fifty-years-of-relief-society/part-1/1-2/1-2-7.

11. April 28, 1842 • Thursday, *The First Fifty Years of Relief Society*.

12. Journal, December 1841–December 1842, 94, The Joseph Smith Papers, https://www.josephsmithpapers.org/paper-summary/journal-december-1841-december-1842/25.

13. History, 1838–1856, volume C-1 [2 November 1838–31 July 1842], 1328–1329, The Joseph Smith Papers, https://www.josephsmithpapers.org/paper-summary/history-1838-1856-volume-c-1-2-november-1838-31-july-1842/502.

14. Heber C. Kimball to Parley P. Pratt and Mary Ann Frost Pratt, June 17, 1842, Church History Library, The Church of Jesus Christ of Latter-day Saints, Salt Lake City.

15. Steven C. Harper, "Freemasonry and the Latter-day Saint Temple Endowment Ceremony," in *A Reason for Faith: Navigating LDS Doctrine and Church History*, edited by Laura Harris Hales (Provo, UT: Religious Studies Center, 2016).

16. May 27, 1842 • Friday, *The First Fifty Years of Relief Society*, https://churchhistorianspress.org/the-first-fifty-years-of-relief-society/part-1/1-2/1-2-11.

17. Russell M. Nelson, "Spiritual Treasures," *Ensign* or *Liahona*, November 2019.

19. Melissa and Benjamin Johnson Learn the New and Everlasting Covenant

1. William to Sally Phelps, May 26, 1835, quoted in Bruce A. Van Orden, ed., "Writing to Zion," *BYU Studies* 33 no. 3 (1993): 6.

2. Parley P. Pratt, *Autobiography of Parley P. Pratt* (1979), 297–98, https://

www.churchofjesuschrist.org/study/ensign/2015/08/he-taught-me-the
-heavenly-order-of-eternity? lang=eng.

3. Benjamin Franklin Johnson, *My Life's Review* (Salt Lake City: Zion's
Printing and Publishing Co., 1947), 96.

4. William Clayton, Journal, May 16, 1843, Church History Library, The
Church of Jesus Christ of Latter-day Saints, Salt Lake City.

5. Discourse, 27 August 1843, as Reported by Willard Richards, 70, The
Joseph Smith Papers, https://www.josephsmithpapers.org/paper-summary
/discourse-27-august-1843-as-reported-by-willard-richards/2.

6. Discourse, 27 August 1843, as Reported by William Clayton, 102, The
Joseph Smith Papers, https://www.josephsmithpapers.org/paper-summary
/discourse-27-august-1843-as-reported-by-william-clayton/1.

7. Discourse, 27 August 1843, as Reported by James Burgess, 16, The
Joseph Smith Papers, https://www.josephsmithpapers.org/paper-summary
/discourse-27-august-1843-as-reported-by-james-burgess/3.

8. Journal, December 1842–June 1844; Book 3, 15 July 1843–29 February
1844, 110, The Joseph Smith Papers, https://www.josephsmithpapers.org
/paper-summary/journal-december-1842-june-1844-book-3-15-july
-1843-29-february-1844/116.

9. George A. Smith, Address, December 1874, *The Millennial Star* 37
(2 February 1875): 66.

10. "Journal (January 1, 1843–December 31, 1844)," January 29, 1844–
January 31, 1844, The Wilford Woodruff Papers, https://www.wilford
woodruffpapers.org/p/GW5.

11. William Clayton, Journal, May 16, 1843, Church History Library, The
Church of Jesus Christ of Latter-day Saints, Salt Lake City; emphasis
added.

20. How Joseph Smith Tasked Brigham
Young to Carry On the Restoration

1. "Journal (January 1, 1841–December 31, 1842)," March 28, 1842–April
2, 1842, The Wilford Woodruff Papers, https://www.wilfordwoodruff
papers.org/p/1zm.

2. Journal, December 1841–December 1842, 94, The Joseph Smith Papers,
https://www.josephsmithpapers.org/paper-summary/journal-december
-1841-december-1842/25.

3. Journal, December 1841–December 1842, 94.

4. See Discourse, between circa 26 June and circa 2 July 1839, as Reported by Willard Richards, 17, The Joseph Smith Papers, https://www.josephsmith papers.org/paper-summary/discourse-between-circa-26-june-and-circa-2 -july-1839-as-reported-by-willard-richards/3.

5. Discourse, 31 August 1842, 82, The Joseph Smith Papers, https://www .josephsmithpapers.org/paper-summary/discourse-31-august-1842/3.

6. Journal, December 1842–June 1844; Book 3, 15 July 1843–29 February 1844, 110, The Joseph Smith Papers, https://www.josephsmithpapers.org /paper-summary/journal-december-1842-june-1844-book-3-15-july -1843-29-february-1844/116.

7. Journal, December 1842–June 1844; Book 3, 15 July 1843–29 February 1844, 113, 122.

8. Journal, December 1842–June 1844; Book 4, 1 March–22 June 1844, 48, The Joseph Smith Papers, https://www.josephsmithpapers.org /paper-summary/journal-december-1842-june-1844-book-4-1-march-22 -june-1844/50.

9. Alexander L. Baugh and Richard Neitzel Holzapfel, "I Roll the Burthen and Responsibility of Leading This Church Off from My Shoulders on to Yours," *BYU Studies Quarterly* 49 no. 3 (2010): 15–19.

10. Baugh and Holzapfel, "I Roll the Burthen and Responsibility."

11. Parley P. Pratt, "Proclamation," [1 Jan. 1845] *Millennial Star* 5 (Mar. 1845): 151.

12. John Nuttall Journal, February 7, 1877, Special Collections, Harold B. Lee Library, Brigham Young University, Provo, Utah.

13. Steven C. Harper, editor, "A Testimony Written by Martha Tuttle Gardner," *Nauvoo Journal* 7 no. 2 (1985): 57–59.

14. "Journal (January 1, 1843 – December 31, 1844)," August 18, 1844, The Wilford Woodruff Papers, https://www.wilfordwoodruffpapers.org/p/P1n.

15. Brigham Young, Journal 1837–1845, Church History Library, The Church of Jesus Christ of Latter-day Saints, Salt Lake City. Quotes are from January 24, 1845 and September 143, 1845.

16. Parley P. Pratt to Isaac Rogers, September 6, 1845, Church History Library, The Church of Jesus Christ of Latter-day Saints, Salt Lake City.

17. B. H. Roberts, *History of the Church of Jesus Christ of Latter-Day Saints Period II*, volume 7, 465.

18. William Clayton, Journal, October 10, 1845–December 7, 1845, Church History Library, The Church of Jesus Christ of Latter-day Saints, Salt Lake

City. Leonard J. Arrington, *Brigham Young: American Moses* (Urbana, IL: University of Illinois Press, 1986), 126. Brigham Young, Diary, January 12, 1846, Church History Library, The Church of Jesus Christ of Latter-day Saints, Salt Lake City.

19. Brigham Young Manuscript History, January 23–February 2, 1846, Church History Library, The Church of Jesus Christ of Latter-day Saints, Salt Lake City.

20. Brigham Young Manuscript History, February 3, 1846, Church History Library, The Church of Jesus Christ of Latter-day Saints, Salt Lake City.

21. Harper, "A Testimony Written by Martha Tuttle Gardner."

21. Continuity, Change, and the Ongoing Restoration

1. "President Young commenced to give the Word and Will of God concerning the emigration of the Saints," Doctrine and Covenants section 136, (Journal History of the Church, January 14, 1847, CR 100 137, Church History Library, The Church of Jesus Christ of Latter-day Saints, Salt Lake City, Utah). Richard E. Bennett, *We'll Find the Place: The Mormon Exodus 1846–1848* (Salt Lake City: Deseret Book, 1997), 70.

2. "Journal (January 1, 1847–December 31, 1853)," February 16, 1847, The Wilford Woodruff Papers, https://wilfordwoodruffpapers.org/p/qx9y.

3. Brigham Young, vision, February 17, 1847, CR 1234 1, Brigham Young Office Files, Church History Library, The Church of Jesus Christ of Latter-day Saints, Salt Lake City.

4. "Journal (January 1, 1873–February 7, 1880)," January 14, 1877–January 18, 1877, The Wilford Woodruff Papers, https://wilfordwoodruffpapers .org/p/BLQY.

5. John Taylor, Minutes of the School of the Prophets, October 1883, Church History Library, The Church of Jesus Christ of Latter-day Saints, Salt Lake City.

6. Wilford Woodruff, 8 April 1894, in Brian H. Stuy, ed., *Collected Discourses*, 5 vols. (Sandy, UT: B. H. S. Publishing, 1987), 4: 72.

7. "The Law of Adoption," *Deseret Evening News*, April 14, 1894, 9.

8. "The Law of Adoption," *Deseret Evening News*. See also "The Law of Adoption," *Messages of the First Presidency of The Church of Jesus Christ of Latter-day Saints*, 6 vols., comp. James R. Clark [1965–75], vol. 3, 254–255; *Saints: The Story of the Church of Jesus Christ in the Latter Days*, vol. 1,

The Standard of Truth, 1815–1846; and Richard E. Bennett, *Temples Rising: A Heritage of Sacrifice* (Salt Lake City: Deseret Book, 2019), 299–300.

9. "The Law of Adoption," *Deseret Evening News*. See also "The Law of Adoption," *Messages of the First Presidency of The Church of Jesus Christ of Latter-day*; *The Discourses of Wilford Woodruff*, sel. G. Homer Durham [1946], 155; *Teaching of Presidents of the Church: Wilford Woodruff* [2004], xxxiii–xxxiv; and Richard E. Bennett, *Temples Rising: A Heritage of Sacrifice*.

10. Richard Neitzel Holzapfel and Steven C. Harper, "'This is My Testimony, Spoken by Myself into a Talking Machine': Wilford Woodruff's 1897 Statement in Stereo," *BYU Studies Quarterly* 45 no. 2 (2006): 112–116, https://byustudies.byu.edu/article/this-is-my-testimony-spoken-by-myself -into-a-talking-machine-wilford-woodruffs-1897-statement-in-stereo/.

11. Russell M. Nelson, "The Temple and Your Spiritual Foundation," *Liahona*, November 2021.

12. Nelson, "The Temple and Your Spiritual Foundation."

13. "First Presidency Statement on Temples," January 2, 2019, newsroom .ChurchofJesusChrist.org.

22. All Are Alike unto God

1. Matt McBride, "Peter," *Century of Black Mormons*, https://exhibits.lib.utah. edu/s/century-of-black-mormons/page/peter.

2. Stephen R. Haynes, *Noah's Curse: The Biblical Justification of American Slavery* (New York: Oxford University Press, 2002).

3. Russell M. Nelson, "Let God Prevail," *Liahona*, November 2020.

4. Kirtland Elders' Certificates, CR 100 401, 61, Church History Library, The Church of Jesus Christ of Latter-day Saints, Salt Lake City, Utah. https://catalog.churchofjesuschrist.org/assets/96f4f1f1-d62d-460a-a317 -13098bc0279b/0/82.

5. W. Paul Reeve, "Elijah Able," *Century of Black Mormons*, https://exhibits .lib.utah.edu/s/century-of-black-mormons/page/able-elijah.

6. Lyle W. Dorset, "Slaveholding in Jackson County, Missouri," *Bulletin of the Missouri Historical Society* 20 no. 1 (October 1963): 25–27.

7. E.S. Adby, *Journal of A Residence and Tour in The United States in North America,* Volume 3 (London: John Murray, 1835), 41–59.

8. W. W. Phelps, "Free People of Color," *The Evening and the Morning Star*, July 1833, 218–219, https://contentdm.lib.byu.edu/digital/collection /NCMP1820-1846/id/28024.

9. William W. Phelps, *The Evening and the Morning Star, Extra*, 16 July 1833.

10. Historian's Office, General Church Minutes, March 26, 1847, Church History Library, The Church of Jesus Christ of Latter-day Saints, Salt Lake City.

11. Brigham Young, "Speech in Joint Session of the Legislature," February 5, 1852, box 48, folder 3, Brigham Young Papers, Church History Library.

12. Gospel Topics, "Race and the Priesthood," topics.ChurchofJesusChrist.org.

13. There is no known record of a revelation or teaching of the restriction being presented to the Saints for common consent. See M. Russell Ballard, "Stay in the Boat and Hold On!," *Ensign* or *Liahona*, November 2014; Jeffrey R. Holland, "'Lord, I Believe,'" *Ensign* or *Liahona*, May 2013; Dieter F. Uchtdorf, "Be Not Afraid, Only Believe," *Ensign* or *Liahona*, November 2015; Robert L. Millet, "What Is Our Doctrine?," *Religious Educator* 4, no. 3 (2003): 15–33; Michael Goodman, "Oh Say, What is Truth," *BYU Studies Quarterly* 60, no. 3 (2021): 1–26; Anthony Sweat, Michael H. MacKay, and Gerrit J. Dirkmaat, "Doctrine: Models to Evaluate Types and Sources of Latter-day Saint Teachings, *Religious Educator* 17, no. 3 (2016): 103.

14. Gospel Topics, "Race and the Priesthood."

15. Neil L. Andersen, "Trial of Your Faith," *Ensign* or *Liahona*, November 2012.

16. Sixty-first Semiannual General Conference of the Church, Monday, October 6, 1890, Salt Lake City, Utah. Reported in *Deseret Evening News*, October 11, 1890, 2.

17. "Approaching Latter-day Saint Doctrine," Church Newsroom, May 4, 2007, https://newsroom.churchofjesuschrist.org/article/approaching-mormon-doctrine.

18. Neil L. Andersen, "Trial of Your Faith," *Ensign* or *Liahona*, November 2012.

19. James Goldberg and Veronica J. Anderson, "Autobiography of Jane Elizabeth Manning James," *BYU Studies Quarterly* 57 no. 4, https://scholarsarchive.byu.edu/byusq/vol57/iss4/8.

20. Jane E. James letter, Salt Lake City, Utah, to John Taylor, December 27, 1884, Church History Library, The Church of Jesus Christ of Latter-day Saints, Salt Lake City, https://catalog.churchofjesuschrist.org/assets/75f4c1ab-d0da-4e63-98ea-d35b93395eea/0/0.

21. James, Jane Elizabeth Manning, A Century of Black Mormons, https://

exhibits.lib.utah.edu/s/century-of-black-mormons/page/james-jane
-elizabeth-manning.

22. Jane E. James letter to Joseph F. Smith, February 7, 1890, Church History
Library, The Church of Jesus Christ of Latter-day Saints, Salt Lake City,
https://catalog.churchofjesuschrist.org/assets/f22ada32-3117-458b-a390
-125f38af1d49#churchofjesuschrist.

23. Jane E. James letter, Salt Lake City, Utah, to John Taylor, December 27,
1884, CR 1 180, Church History Library, The Church of Jesus Christ
of Latter-day Saints, Salt Lake City; and Quincy D. Newell, *Your Sister
in the Gospel: The Life of Jane Manning James, a Nineteenth-Century Black
Mormon* (New York: Oxford University Press, 2019), 104–118.

24. James Goldberg and Veronica J. Anderson, "Autobiography of Jane
Elizabeth Manning James." Elder M. Russell Ballard quoted Jane and retold
her story in his 2017 general conference talk, "The Trek Continues."

23. The Long-Promised Day

1. See Russell M. Nelson, "Let God Prevail," *Liahona*, November 2020;
and Dallin H. Oaks, "Racism and Other Challenges," BYU Devotional,
October 27, 2020, https://speeches.byu.edu/talks/dallin-h-oaks/racism
-other-challenges/.

2. George A. Smith Family Papers extract from George F. Richards record of
decisions by the Council of the First Presidency and the Twelve Apostles,
cited in W. Paul Reeve, "Race, the Priesthood, and Temples," *Raising the
Standard of Truth*, 428.

3. See statement of the First Presidency of The Church of Jesus Christ of
Latter-day Saints, August 17, 1949, Archives, The Church of Jesus Christ
of Latter-day Saints, Salt Lake City.

4. Joseph Fielding Smith to Alfred M. Nelson, January 31, 1907, MS 14591,
Church History Library, The Church of Jesus Christ of Latter-day Saints,
Salt Lake City, https://catalog.churchofjesuschrist.org/assets/317076f6
-261b-49cd-b37e-1bf8642c1a06/0/0.

5. See Gospel Topics, "Race and the Priesthood," topics.ChurchofJesusChrist
.org.

6. Brigham Young, "Speech in Joint Session of the Legislature," February 5,
1852, box 48, folder 3, Brigham Young Papers, Church History Library,
The Church of Jesus Christ of Latter-day Saints, Salt Lake City.

7. W. Paul Reeve, "Race, the Priesthood, and Temples," *Raising the Standard*

of Truth: Exploring the History and Teachings of the Early Restoration, (Salt Lake City: BYU Religious Studies Center and Deseret Book, 2020), https://rsc.byu.edu/raising-standard-truth/race-priesthood-temples.

8. Journal (October 22, 1865–December 31, 1872), The Wilford Woodruff Papers, accessed February 2, 2024, https://wilfordwoodruffpapers.org/p/kRRN.

9. Stephen R. Haynes, *Noah's Curse: The Biblical Justification of American Slavery* (New York: Oxford University Press, 2002).

10. See William McCary council meeting minutes, Winter Quarters, CR 100 318; 1847 December 2–7, CR 100 318; Brigham Young, Speech to Utah Territorial Legislature, January 23, 1852; and Brigham Young, Speech to Utah Territorial Legislature, February 5, 1852, all at the Church History Library, The Church of Jesus Christ of Latter-day Saints, Salt Lake City, Utah.

11. Orson Pratt, Speech in Utah Constitutional Convention, March 22, 1856, Church History Library, The Church of Jesus Christ of Latter-day Saints, Salt Lake City.

12. B. H. Roberts, *The Contributor* 6 (1885): 296–7.

13. Gospel Topics, "Race and Priesthood," topics.ChurchofJesusChrist.org.

14. Joseph Fielding Smith to Alfred M. Nelson, January 13, 1907, Church History Library, The Church of Jesus Christ of Latter-day Saints, Salt Lake City, https://catalog.churchofjesuschrist.org/assets/317076f6-261b-49cd-b37e-1bf8642c1a06/0/0? lang=eng.

15. Edward L. Kimball, ed., *The Teachings of Spencer W. Kimball: Twelfth President of the Church of Jesus Christ of Latter-day Saints* (Salt Lake City: Bookcraft, 1982), 448–49.

16. Appendix 1 in *Lengthening Our Stride: Globalization of the Church*, ed., Reid L. Neilson and Wayne D. Crosby (Provo, UT: Religious Studies Center; Salt Lake City: Deseret Book, 2017).

17. "Revelation: 'A Continuous Melody and a Thunderous Appeal,'" *Teachings of Presidents of the Church: Spencer W. Kimball*, (Salt Lake City: The Church of Jesus Christ of Latter-day Saints, 2006).

18. Edward L. Kimball, "Spencer W. Kimball and the Revelation on Priesthood," *BYU Studies Quarterly* 47, no. 2 (2008): 7–78.

19. David B. Haight, as quoted in E. Dale LeBaron, "Revelation on the Priesthood," *The Heavens Are Open* (Salt Lake City: Deseret Book, 1993), 199–200.

20. "Revelation: 'A Continuous Melody and a Thunderous Appeal.'"
21. "Be One—A Celebration of the Revelation on the Priesthood," https://www
    .churchofjesuschrist.org/media/video/2018-06-1000-be-one-a-celebration
    -of-the-revelation-on-the-priesthood? lang=eng.
22. Bruce R. McConkie, "All Are Alike unto God," BYU Speeches, August 18,
    1978, https://speeches.byu.edu/talks/bruce-r-mcconkie/alike-unto-god/.
23. McConkie, "All Are Alike unto God."
24. W. Paul Reeve, "Race, the Priesthood, and Temples," *Raising the Standard
    of Truth: Exploring the History and Teachings of the Early Restoration*, (Provo:
    BYU Religious Studies Center and Salt Lake City: Deseret Book, 2020),
    https://rsc.byu.edu/raising-standard-truth/race-priesthood-temples.
25. See Alice Faulkner Burch, ed., *My Lord, He Calls Me: Stories of Faith by
    Black American Latter-day Saints* (Salt Lake City: Deseret Book, 2022).
26. Jeffrey R. Holland, "'Lord, I Believe,'" *Ensign* or *Liahona*, May 2013.
27. Russell M. Nelson, "Let God Prevail," *Liahona*, November 2020.

Epilogue: Why This Church Matters

1. J. Devn Cornish, "The True Church: 'For the Perfecting of the Saints,'"
   Liahona, September 2018.
2. "Kartartismos," Blue Letter Bible, https://www.blueletterbible.org/lexicon
   /g2677/kjv/tr/0-1/.
3. See Russell M. Nelson, "The Power of Spiritual Momentum," *Liahona*, May
   2022.
4. Truman G. Madsen, "The Savior, The Sacrament, and Self-Worth," presented at BYU Women's Conference, Brigham Young University, Provo,
   Utah, Apr. 29, 1999.
5. Journal, 1835–1836, 23, The Joseph Smith Papers, https://www.joseph
   smithpapers.org/paper-summary/journal-1835-1836/24? p=24.
6. Russell M. Nelson, "Peacemakers Needed," *Liahona*, May 2023.